The Coaching Revolution

The Coaching Revolution

How Visionary
Managers Are Using
Coaching to Empower People
and Unlock Their Full Potential

DAVID LOGAN, PH.D., & JOHN KING

Adams Media
Avon, Massachusetts

Dedication

To Thomas Jefferson, Gary Larson, and Adam Smith for their core values—

Jefferson for his dedication to the "noble cause,"
Larson for his sense of humor,
and Smith for his concern with integrity in open markets.

We imagine them sitting at coffee together and saying collectively,
"Do something worthwhile, have a good time doing it, and make some money."

Published by
Adams Media, an F+W Publications Company
57 Littlefield Street, Avon, MA 02322 U.S.A.
www.adamsmedia.com

ISBN: 1-59337-078-4

Printed in the United States of America.

J I H G F E D C B A

Library of Congress Cataloging-in-Publication Data
Logan, David Colman.
The coaching revolution : how visionary managers are using
coaching to empower people and unlock their full potential. / David
Colman Logan and John Paul King.
p. cm.
ISBN 1-58062-485-5 (hardcover) 1-59337-078-4 (paperback)
1. Employee—Counseling of. 2. Employee motivation. 3. Employee
empowerment. 4. Employees—Training of. I. King, John Paul II. Title.
HF5549.5.C8 L64 2001
658.3'14—dc21   2001022616

This publication is designed to provide accurate and authoritative information with regard to
the subject matter covered. It is sold with the understanding that the publisher is not engaged
in rendering legal, accounting, or other professional advice. If legal advice or other expert
assistance is required, the services of a competent professional person should be sought.
—From a *Declaration of Principles* jointly adopted by a Committee of the
American Bar Association and a Committee of Publishers and Associations

Many of the designations used by manufacturers and sellers to distinguish their products are
claimed as trademarks. Where those designations appear in this book and Adams Media was
aware of a trademark claim, the designations have been printed with initial capital letters.

This book is available at quantity discounts for bulk purchases.
For information call 1-800-872-5627.

Interior Illustration by Eric Mueller

Contents

Foreword

By Kathleen Calcidise

In my current role as Chief Operating Officer (Retail) for Apple, and in my past role as President of Virgin Megastores, I oversee one of the most varied groups of people imaginable—people who create art and people who manage operations, people who drive to work in BMWs working alongside people who use inline skates to get to work, people who believe that the essence of business is reflected by a financial statement and people who believe that business just gets in the way.

Like all people who manage, I spend my day solving problems and working toward corporate objectives along the way. The problems include good employees who leave, managers who learn obscure new rules to manage new generations, and executives who struggle to stay ahead of increasingly innovative competitors.

By far the greatest challenge I face is getting this diverse group of talented people to work together. I've found that if I can do that, most of the objectives and problems tend to solve themselves. The ruling paradox of my management experience is that getting people to work together has never been harder. For the first time in American history, managers have access to four major generations in the workplace at the same time—Matures, Boomers, Gen-Xers and the emerging Generation Y.

Putting all this diversity together brings us to the newest problem/opportunity for management. The business world now operates on Internet Time. Because of this phenomenon, managers need quick and effective ways to "mass-customize" their management of employees. It is essential that work management be tailored for individuals in each generation. Managers must become sensitive to and effective with different human categories of specific skills, interests, and values. Each person needs slightly different types and amounts of value-added management.

When we treat employees like they're all the same, they leave. Or worse, they keep pulling a paycheck without giving back much effort.

This is why I believe in coaching—it gives managers proven tools to work with people as individuals. Coaching gets at solving basic issues that managers face—issues that determine how people work with their colleagues, with managers, and with customers.

When managers become manager-coaches, almost anything is possible. I've seen productivity jump, people start working toward common objectives, and good performers become great.

In my experience, most senior managers honestly believe in the principle of releasing people's potential. Yet most managers only pay lip service to this vital element. Actually, releasing potential is an advanced management skill. I believe that in this matter, coaching is the solution. I'd much rather hire someone two years away from being effective than someone who is ten years in and thinks they know all the answers. I look for the spark, the talent. Coaching unlocks that latent ability and brings it into the workplace.

The basic problem, though, is that people full of potential often start their career working in environments where there is *one* way to do things. Without even realizing that there's another way, managers often teach what they were taught—and the cycle of "one way management" continues into the next generation. Soon, people so full of potential become the people who stymie the potential of new hires.

Changing these patterns—*really* changing them—requires a period of instability. *The Coaching Revolution* presents this more clearly than any other business book I've read. It presents an honest picture of why old cycles continue, and what we as managers can do to make change real and permanent.

More importantly, this book also presents what to do about something most managers have known for a long time: people don't work for money. People work to "make a difference." Clichés aside, most of us are in search of our "noble cause." This book will help you to help your employees find theirs, and link it to their jobs.

The Coaching Revolution also gives a deeply insightful overview of the differences between generations. Rather than the commonly accepted stereotyping of people based on age, this book presents what's really different about each generation, and how underneath it all, people are still people.

Most importantly, this book pulls all these threads together. From cover to cover, the book gives concrete tools to see people accurately, spot the areas of untapped potential, and help employees to release it.

The challenge in dealing with employees today is to coach them, not to constrain them. These people are our future. They stimulate all of us to higher levels of thinking. *The Coaching Revolution* shows managers a powerful and effective way to help our employees become the star performers they deserve to be.

Introduction

When Jim Beasley entered the doors of a medium-sized company in the Southeast, he didn't think of himself as a revolutionary. He thought he was just there to provide a new kind of business consulting that focused on individual development. He was there as a coach.

People like Jim are revolutionaries, as are the people who hire them. Just a few decades ago, good leadership was defined as the ability to give and receive orders. People didn't have the potential to maximize; they were cogs in the great industrial machines that were fighting the Cold War.

Even earlier, Henry Ford "proved" that the best method for running a company is to chop up jobs until each person has a very specific task along the assembly line. "Bolt welder #3" maximized his potential by welding every #3 bolt exactly the same way. If he didn't, his supervisor would step in to make sure the #3 bolt got proper welding.

Today, company executives are beginning to realize that the short-comings of the past have created a kind of slave labor in America: people are too often valued only for their ability to do a specific job.

Even many college-educated professionals feel like Dilbert—they are in the prison of their cubicle and their job description.

Just as every revolution begins with a felt sense of injustice, executives, managers, and employees are waking up to the fact that organizations are wasting billions of dollars in human capital.

The employees feel exploited. The managers feel they don't have the resources they need. The executives feel the company can't change fast enough to keep up with increasingly innovative competition.

The leaders of the revolution are coming from several areas. Savvy executives are launching programs to unlock the potential in their managers and employees. Talented people from diverse backgrounds are training themselves to become professional coaches.

Yet the changes are not just coming from the outside. Today, managers are giving up the old "command and control" model for the coaching model. As evidence that things have changed—and that the changes are just beginning—Jack Welch recently said that in the future, people who are not coaches will not be promoted. Managers who are coaches will be the norm, he predicted.

This book is written to managers who recognize that things are changing, and who want to become coaches for the people they manage.

Those executives who embrace coaching as a way of life are seeing bottom-line improvements in their companies. Those managers who are hiring or becoming coaches for the people they manage are seeing their careers take off. Those employees fortunate enough to have access to coaching are finding fulfilling jobs and lives. As the revolution moves forward, those who choose to join are benefiting. Welcome to the coaching revolution.

And the revolution is just beginning.

chapter one

"What the Hell Is Coaching?"

"So, what can I help you with?" the coach asked over his headphones, leaning back in his chair.

"My business is in the toilet," the potential client replied, his voice both irritated and anxious. "Creditors are after me, my salespeople aren't performing. A friend thought you could help."

"What's your business?" the coach replied casually.

"Selling telecommunications to small businesses," the client responded, wondering if this discussion would lead anywhere, or if he'd have to file for Chapter 11.

"And why did you pick this business?" the coach asked in a tone that made this sound like the only reasonable question in the world.

"Because I did it for five years working for someone else." This was getting frustrating, he thought. "I'm an entrepreneur—of course I hate working for other people."

"So what's changed?"

The man sighed. "I want to sell these telecom services to small businesses, because I know there are a lot of them." He had just stated the obvious, for at least the fortieth time in the last two weeks of talking to people about his problems. So far, the conversations had had only netted trivial advice—such as making sure his list of potential customers was up to date.

"And when you worked for someone else, did you sell to large or small companies?"

"Large, but the idiot I worked for didn't know that there are more small businesses than large."

"So you're running a business that you've never proven can work, and you've abandoned an idea that made your ex-boss a lot of money?"

Silence. "I suppose that's one way of looking at it."

"Given that, what should you consider doing?" the coach asked, wondering if his client had seen the problem yet.

"I suppose I should sell to large businesses, at least for a while."

"Yep," the coach replied.

"I feel really stupid," the man responded. "Like *DUH!*"

"Don't," the coach replied. "We all have blind spots. My job is to help you explore how you can look into yours and become more effective. You connected the dots. I just asked the questions. Now—what are you going to do differently moving forward?"

"Well, first thing is I'm going to meet with my salespeople and refocus them on larger companies."

"And when will you do this?" the coach asked, still leaning back in his chair.

"By this Friday at noon."

"Good. You and I should talk after your meeting. How about Friday at 1:00?"

"Friday at 1:00 it is."

We have had the opportunity to consult and coach to businesses from start-ups to the world's largest employers—for a collective 40 years. Over this period, we've read just about every book on coaching that's ever been written—including several not yet published. We've spoken to tens of thousands of people, from front-line employees to senior executives in *Fortune* 500 companies, and because of this rich input from so many people over time, we've had the opportunity to see for ourselves what works and what doesn't.

Our experience is that the best solutions aren't complicated, but they also aren't simplistic. They are "brilliantly simple." They cut through the clutter of a situation and reveal the real issue and a technique for solving it quickly. The entrepreneur in the preceding real example had heard all the simplistic solutions he could stomach—from "watch your cash flow" to "follow your instincts." And he'd heard the complicated advice—such as "perform a demographic analysis of your target market to verify your business plan assumptions."

He needed what most people need: a brilliantly simple solution. This book is written for managers to help them coach their employees toward these sorts of solutions.

That said, this book boils coaching down into three things. These three elements are the cornerstones to coaching.

The first element is "see." Coaching involves helping people to see a problem differently, or to realize how they're not acting consistently with their goals. When the entrepreneur discovered this for himself, he uttered a magic word—*duh*. We'll get to *duh* later. It's a word, like its cousins *aha* and *wow*, that you'll hear a lot from people as you coach them. It's a sign that the world just changed for them, that they finally see a way out of their problem.

The second element is "say." For thousands of years, people have known that if you can get someone to say what they're going to do, they're much more likely to follow through with it. In coaching, once people have an insight—and say a word like *duh*—they usually won't do anything with this insight unless the coach guides them to articulate a specific goal—what they're going to do and when they're going to do it.

The third element is "do." Even when people say they're going to take an action, they often won't. The coach holds them accountable for what they say. The entrepreneur in the above example probably won't accomplish his goals perfectly in his Friday meeting. So a coach will follow up to check up on his progress and help him "see" how he was effective and how he wasn't. Then the process starts over again.

See, say, and do. It's the formula that great coaches have used for thousands of years to help people shift from average to amazing.

But we're getting ahead of ourselves.

When we talk about coaching to executives, the most common response is: "What the hell is coaching? Is it the next fad everyone will laugh at in five years?" An automotive executive, much experienced with training, asked us if this is the new term that consultants use to sell the same old stuff under a new buzz phrase. This is actually a good question.

If we told the executives that coaching is *see, say,* and *do,* they'd probably respond by calling security. Then we wouldn't have interesting stories to relate in this book—or houses to live in. So, let's start with a brief history of coaching.

When coaching first began to catch on in companies, outside coaches were hired to introduce this new management *du jour* (as some cynics called it) into the company's culture. When it was done right, the results amazed people—even the cynics. The sharp ones realized that coaching was a tool that was destined to change everything in companies. They wanted to learn these skills themselves, to become "manager-coaches."

Since you're already clued in, you know that manager-coaches work with people until they "see" a clear picture of how to unlock their potential (or the potential of their companies). You'll know it's happened because people say one of those magic words we'll talk about in the next chapter. Words like *duh.*

But are the cynics right? Is this the next fad in management that everyone will laugh at in five years? Is it the next fodder for *Dilbert* cartoons?

Coaching isn't new. It has been with us for as long as humans have had the desire to improve. In fact, it's one of the oldest studies in human civilization. It comes to us from the same people who thought of some other really nifty ideas—like democracy, geometry, medicine, and logic. We're talking about the Greeks.

The Greeks were interested in lots of things, including sports. And they—like any university today with a good sports program—invested heavily in figuring out how to make good athletes into champions. They turned to experts in boosting performance. These experts were called coaches.

Coaching was the process that turned gifted natural athletes into champions who won it all in the ancient Olympic games. Today, every contender in the modern Olympics surrounds herself with coaches.

The reason for coaching in sports is obvious: people who want to become the best in the world need individualized attention from experts. It's not enough to learn general principles or just gather more information. Champions need people to show them where they aren't realizing their full potential. Then they need the same people to guide them through the process of turning potential into performance gains.

Business leaders are finally realizing what sports experts have known for thousands of years: individualized attention from an expert is the only way to unlock a person's full ability.[1] We recently told a biotechnology executive the story of coaching. When he realized that business is only now learning what sports has known for nearly 3,000 years, he responded with one of our favorite words. "I *see* it now."

E. Kay Stepp was the first woman to ever run a public utility. She abandoned that prestigious position to go into business by herself as a corporate coach. She recently told *Inc.* magazine, "What I'm trying to do is to remove the blind spots."[2] Yet people can get very defensive about their blind spots—some people even deny that they have any blind spots at all.

E. Kay Stepp brings us to the most basic principle for becoming a manager-coach: creating an open and safe relationship with employees so they can begin to see their mistakes, admit their weaknesses, and talk about their potential that is, so far, just potential.

An Environment Safe for Coaching

If you're serious about becoming a manager-coach, congratulations. The benefits to you, to your employees, and to your business are enough to turn a bankruptcy-in-the-making into solvency. The prerequisite to learning the tips and techniques in this book is that you have to create what communication experts call a "relational context" in which anything can be said without penalty.

Coauthor Dave Logan thought he communicated pretty well. He had four degrees in communication, including a Ph.D. from one of the top programs in the country. He was a professor in a major business school where he taught, among other things, communication. He was gaining a reputation as a keynote speaker and workshop leader in all areas of communication. One day, over dinner, his friend of ten years told him that he "never listened." If he were a more humble guy, he would have thought about it and said "*duh*," realizing that his wife was offering some valuable advice. Instead, he started listing off his degrees and accomplishments, proving, beyond all doubt, that he did, in fact, listen.

The next day, he told the story to coauthor John King, thinking that John would reassure him that, of course, he listened. After all, Dave had the degrees to prove it. To Dave's surprise, John laughed. And his next words gripped Dave like a great white shark: "She's right, you don't."

Creating an environment that is safe is like listening—most of us think we do it. Most of us can even point to proof that we do it all the time. Yet most employees report that their bosses don't listen to them, that it's not safe to talk about a weakness, and that the gates of hell would devour them if they ever asked for coaching.

Creating an environment safe for coaching is the hardest step in this book, because most of us think we can do it already. Unless you've been trained to create this kind of environment, you probably can't do it yet.

That leads us back to Jim Beasley, the business coach from the Introduction. When he entered the doors of a medium-sized company in the Southeast, he had no idea that the key to turning this place around would come down to creating an environment that allowed the individual to release his or her gifts and talents into the workplace.

As a trained coach, he knew the importance of setting the environment. As a condition of working with the company, Jim asked that the president go on record as saying that everything people told Jim would remain strictly confidential. In an address to management, the president said that he completely trusted Jim and that he knew Jim wouldn't repeat anything the employees told him.

At first employees discussed simple issues—fights with their bosses, dealing with a corporate culture that had become closed and uncommunicative. As time went on, the employees trusted Jim more and more. They began to discuss deeper and more personal issues—their problems at home, their concerns about whether they were really in the right job, and their negative feelings about the company.

As the issues deepened, Jim listened closely, much as a therapist would. He empathized with their concerns, but more importantly, he listened so that they would "see" things for themselves. Once they did— and a *duh* or an *aha* came out—Jim encouraged them to use these insights to make important and permanent changes in how they did their jobs and connected with people.

Jim recalls one turning point in this company. A senior manager was angry with the president of the company. After she vented her frustrations, Jim facilitated a discussion in which she realized that she needed to tell the president her concerns. Jim then worked with her until she could tell the story without seeming to blame the president. Jim had also been coaching the president and management to listen and really hear what was being said.

The next day, the senior manager went to see the president. She spoke frankly of her concerns and explained exactly what changes she thought needed to be made. Because of the president's commitment to the growth and development of the individual, Jim's coaching, and her own courage, she and the president were able to have a safe, open, and honest discussion. Out of that discussion came important and positive changes that helped move the company to a new level.

Through these positive moves, the company's morale improved and the team atmosphere was restored. All the employees (over 100) benefited. *Wow!*

When working with a manager who was told to find solutions "or else," coach Jackie Nagel first established an atmosphere of openness and trust. She then helped the manager see his own potential and plan specific actions that would improve the operations of his team. Over time, Jackie coached this manager to become a better communicator—now he, himself, could establish openness and trust. She also taught him to facilitate cooperative planning and to listen intensely, just as she had done with him. In short, Jackie trained the manager in the basics of coaching.

Once the manager became a coach for his employees, he provided individual attention to them until they became coaches for each other. The employees also became effective coaches for the manager. The whole time, Jackie was coaching him.

The effect of this downstream flow of coaching skills was that the entire group's communication pattern, style of planning, and method of responding to problems shifted. Employees still had complaints, but the manager began using even these in a more constructive way.

By creating an environment that is safe for insight and change, you can facilitate results like these for your company. Before going deeper into how you can manage your relational contexts, we need to answer a question. In the words of one well-placed human resources vice president, "Can't we get there with something that's more proven—like training?" Good question—we're glad you asked.

Why Not Just Use Training?

For the last several years, the solution of choice to manager and employee skill deficits was training.

As an industry, training has exploded in the last 20 years, according to research by the American Society of Training and Development. Motorola University studied America's largest companies and found that the average spends 1 percent of its overall budget on employee training. Progressive companies, including Hewlett-Packard and Intel, spend an average of 3 percent.

Why training?

Training is based on the model of the classroom, so it's familiar to educated people. It's relatively low risk, since most people don't radically change their behavior after a group training session. Training is also easy to control, since supervisors in the company can pre-approve course content. In short, training is an inexpensive and easy approach to employee development.

But does it work?

The classroom model makes sense when people are learning a new skill. However, as people's skill levels increase, it becomes much more difficult for them to improve, since they require time-consuming, individual attention from experts to fine-tune their newly acquired skills.

To use an analogy, a single college professor can teach 200 undergraduates the basics of chemistry. A senior-level class will have 50 students. An early graduate course will have 25 students. A doctorate-level class will have five students. Eventually, the student works on a dissertation and has a committee of three or four professors. The teachers now outnumber the student. This is the kind of attention it takes to make someone world-class.

Corporations need their key people to become world-class, but companies seldom get beyond a classroom training model that assumes people don't need individual attention. This is the weakness of the training model.

In the days of Henry Ford, when people were in very narrow jobs, training could teach hundreds of people to do their jobs at once. During the 1960s and '70s, when management was largely about giving and taking orders, the mass training model still sufficed: a company could still orient large groups to new policies, or teach them the basics of new skills.

Today, managers and employees have to refine and redefine their skills to become global leaders in their fields. This requires a model that is more intensive and more focused than training.

To put it bluntly, training alone is unable to unlock the potential of employees and managers. It usually fails to make us "see" our potential, "say" what we're going to do, and hold us accountable to make sure we "do" it.

To survive intensifying competition, companies—and their employees—need much more than traditional training. People need the individualized attention from experts that will enable them to build better careers, happier lives, and stronger relationships.

Training has gotten us this far, but now we need coaching.

By creating a safe working environment and learning the techniques of *see*, *say*, *do*, you can become a manager-coach. The payoffs for you are many: you'll be better able to deal with common problems in the workplace, the morale of your team will rise, your employee retention rates will increase. We've also found that manager-coaches are generally happier, since the workplace is calmer, people are developing their skills, and the company is moving forward. When managers become manager-coaches, everyone wins.

part one

See

When discussing the coaching revolution, Marie Antoinette may not be the first person who comes to mind. Her very name conjures up the infamous words "let them eat cake" that she uttered during a time when her people were growing hungry and angry. Her thoughtless words were a symptom of a much deeper failing.

Only fourteen years old when her family sent her to France to assume the formidable role of the future queen, Marie was naive and unprepared for leadership.

Burdened by the pain of a backstabbing court and a loveless marriage, she chose to ignore her mounting problems by amusing herself in games and extravagant living. As long as she could not see the growing resentment of her people crippled by starvation and taxation, to her it did not exist. She became oblivious to criticism, even to blatant attacks.

She might have had the potential to be a great leader, yet any ability and charisma she possessed were thwarted by her inability to see her gaping blind spots. In her mind, it was always the people's fault. They were the ones who were rude. They were disloyal and disrespectful. They were out of control. And, in the end, it was these people who devised her downfall and death.[1]

Many of us are walking Marie Antoinettes when it comes to seeing what holds us back from realizing our full potential and noticing the danger signs ahead.

Seeing is the first step in coaching. A good manager-coach will get individuals to see the gap in their own performance. It's not enough for others to see it. People don't change until they see the need to.

If you read on, you may help others see some things they never intended to see. But only by helping them see will they grasp their fullest potential and avoid unhappy outcomes. In the long run these insights will make them more effective at achieving championship results.

The next four chapters will provide manager-coaches with the tools to hack through the facade that covers our unrealized potential. You will learn how to make the environment at work safe for coaching, how to listen like a coach to help others see, how to clean up the office trash, and how to assess your and your employees' work-life impact. You will gain new insights into how to break down those barriers that blind us as to our full potential.

chapter two

A Coach's Four
Favorite Words

Recently, we coached the owners of a small business who were having trouble—big trouble. The company was losing money, sales were spiraling down, and it appeared that the president of the company was embezzling money.

As the CEO of the company said at a pause in our meeting, "Other than the fact that we're in death throes because our president has killed our company, everything's great."

The owners wanted revenge—pure and simple. They wanted to hold the sales manager up to be publicly humiliated for what they called "the sales spiral of death." They wanted evidence that the president had walked away with about $200,000 so that they could "make his life a living hell" with one lawsuit after another. Most importantly, they wanted the accountant's "head on a platter" (their words) for allowing these events to happen.

One of the owners—who also sat on the board—pulled us aside and asked us to find evidence of collusion between these three people. "It would make me feel a lot better," he said, "if I knew there were a conspiracy going on."

We looked at each other and said, almost in unison, "Huh?"

"Look," he said, his eyes rolling back. "It's one thing to be slimed by one person. It makes you feel dumb. But I wouldn't feel so dumb if I knew these guys were working together."

Again, "Huh?"

"I'd just feel better. Please, spend some time and find some evidence."

John spoke up first. "So, what you're saying is that the company is in terrible shape, may go bankrupt, and you want us to spend our time finding evidence to make you feel better."

"Right. Thanks for understanding," he said with a reassured tone in his voice. He turned to walk back into the meeting.

John interrupted his escape plan. "So instead of building the company back up, you want us to run up our fees soothing your self-esteem?" he asked.

"Can't you do both?" His face turned to surprise.

"If we spend our time trying to make you feel better, the company will die and all these people will lose their jobs. Paul, you can't make the weak strong by making the strong weak."

Paul thought about it for a few seconds. At first he seemed disappointed. Then a look of understanding spread across his face. "Okay, I guess I was just coming up with something to tell my wife. I don't want her to think I'm stupid."

"Paul, what will she think if you hire us—at a big chunk of money—just to give you a tale about why you weren't stupid for losing the first chunk of money?" John asked.

"I guess she'd say I was being stupid again."

We looked at him for another moment of awkward silence.

"*Duh,*" he finally said, turning to walk away.

Duh is one of our favorite words. It's a sign that people have taken the first step in the coaching process—that they "see" things differently. Our other favorite words are *aha, wow,* and *shazam*. Ben Cohen, the cofounder of Ben & Jerry's said that "people only change when the need for change becomes self-evident."[1] *Duh* is a sign that the need for change has become self-evident.

In our time helping managers grow into manager-coaches, it's always amazing to us how people use *duh*, *aha*, and *wow* in similar ways. It's as though we've all been secretly abducted by space aliens and taught this vocabulary in our sleep.

Duh is what people say when there's something they haven't seen that's important—a "dog that didn't bark." When they add this element that has been absent, they defeat problems that have prevented them from accomplishing their goals. It's when the entrepreneur sees that he's spending his time in ways that won't make money, when he's ignoring proven sources of revenue.

Aha is a step up from *duh*. It's what people say when they learn a new insight, a tool or technique that complements what they already know. With this addition, they can move to the next level of managerial effectiveness. We recently worked with a good manager who realized she could become a great manager by listening—*really* listening—to her people. She was a great delegator and strategic thinker, but listened to the little voice in her head rather than the pleas for help from her people. She sat down in her chair as if we'd explained the grand unification theory of physics. "*Aha!*" she said, her eyes wide with excitement.

Wow is a level beyond *aha*. People say it when they see the big picture—a vision that propels their business and career into warp speed. The same manager—who two years later was now a vice president—realized that her departments were the only ones operating as a genuine team, and that the entire company needed to operate the same way—or the competition would either bury them or buy them out. A vision of a very different company gelled in her mind—the solution to 90 percent of the organization's critical problems. In that second, she realized that it wouldn't happen unless she led the change—as the corporation's next CEO.

Shazam is a word we don't hear very often, but one we hope you will say while reading this book. It's the feeling that—depending on your view of things—God, the universe, the Force, or Fate—has given you a thought that will change everything. It's what happened when Einstein dreamt about the key to relativity, when Henry Ford caught a glimpse of the modern assembly line, when Walt Disney thought of a park of happy—and well-paying—customers.

We believe that the first coaching step in getting people to "see" is to work with them until they have one of these experiences—and *duh, aha, wow,* or *shazam* pops out of their mouths. If the coaching is great, they might even say them one after the other.

But how can we get people to see these insights in the first place? It won't happen if the environment is hostile, as we talked about in Chapter 1. The second key step to getting people to "see" is to listen like a coach.

Listening Is Believing

Yogi Berra, one of the great wise men of the twentieth century, once said, "You can observe a lot just by watching."

For people who pay attention, this cross-wired sentence packs a wallop—lots of people observe, but not as many truly watch. Plenty of people have excellent eyesight, but that doesn't mean they see what's in front of them.

It's the same with listening. If Yogi were to make a statement about listening, he might say: "You can hear a lot just by listening." Sure, it still sounds a little oddball. But we've noticed a huge difference between the way coaches listen and the way most people listen. When managers apply the listening skills of top coaches, their departments will change dramatically—and very much for the better.

Shiny Objects

Fish and birds have one thing in common: they're both attracted to shiny objects. This is why lures are often glittery and why crows' nests sometimes contain bits of aluminum foil and Christmas tinsel.

How well do most people listen? Not very, for the most part. Instead, when another person is speaking, the listener's mind becomes like a crow's, surveying the terrain looking for something that catches their attention—something that attracts them—something shiny. This usually means that our thoughts wander completely away from the other person. We may think about lunch, money, TV shows, or sex. Or we may be thinking about what we want to say as soon as the person stops talking. The more boring we think the person and his topic is to us, the more our minds will hunt for something attractive to think and talk about. Like birds and fish, our listening is drawn to the shiny object.

Think back to college. Did you master the art of yawning with your mouth closed? As someone who taught college for ten years, coauthor Dave Logan knows the signs through thousands of hours of careful observation. The lips remain closed but the mouth opens ever so slightly. The eyes turn inward, then, like a tsunami crashing into the shore, the yawn hits—the nostrils flare, the neck muscles tighten, and the chin quivers. After about three seconds, the storm passes. If the person is an expert in the art of the closed-mouth yawn, he'll quickly show that he is, in fact, riveted by the subject—he'll take at least ten seconds worth of notes and then nod slightly, indicating his agreement with the professor.

The closed-mouth yawn often happens when we're so bored by the subject that we pretend to listen, but our mind is light years away. Most sociable people have learned how to seem to pay attention—to show the "nonverbals" of listening—while in reality they're on a mental hunt for shiny objects. This is *not* how coaches listen.

There's a slightly higher level of listening that still is *not* how coaches listen.

Patella Reflexes

While we're waiting for our turn to say something, we may hear the other person's words quite well—this is what happens when we train ourselves to concentrate on the discussion rather than hunt for shiny objects.

Here's a typical workplace example. Sheila might say, "The client asked for changes to the delivery schedule, and now I have to change all the distribution routes." Perhaps Bob then responds, "Man, I just hate this place. Why can't the salespeople nail down the right schedules when they close their deals?"

Bob's response suggests that he heard Sheila's words just fine. But what did Bob listen to? Sheila mentioned changing distribution routes, and Bob responded by complaining about the salespeople.

What happened? This is another listening problem, different from the hunt for shiny objects.

As part of a routine physical, a doctor will usually tap just below the knees with a small rubber hammer. If our reflexes are normal, we'll kick the air, ever so slightly. This is the Patella Reflex. If the hunt for shiny objects is the first big problem in listening, the Patella Reflex is the second.

It should be simple to see that while Bob heard Sheila, he listened until she said something that tapped his Patella Reflex. Then he waited for his turn to talk. Bob *thinks* that he and Sheila share a gripe about salespeople failing to nail down the details of contracts and delivery schedules. Bob listened to Sheila's statement through a filter. Unfortunately for Bob, he doesn't know that he has this filter. Worse yet, we're all a bunch of Bobs.

The fact that these filters exist isn't a problem. In fact, listening without a filter is impossible.[2] Frankly, many filters serve a useful purpose. The problem is that people are usually not aware that these filters exist. The result is that most conversations don't really connect people—they actually drive people apart. One person speaks until the other person's filter causes him to object, agree, or think of an example—in other words, until his Patella Reflex is activated.

If you've ever watched daytime talk shows, you know this is true—the only difference being that melodrama underscores the point. A person faced with some problem will sit in a chair on the stage. One radical thought after another will flow from his or her mouth. The people in the audience—all riveted by the performance on the stage—wait until their Patella Reflex is hit. Then they wave their arms in the air as a signal to the host with the cordless microphone that they have something to say. When their turn comes and they have the mike, it's their job to say something that will strike the Patella Reflex of more people. The more Patella Reflexes hit, the more successful the show (at least in terms of ratings).

We see unchecked, interpretive filters—and the resulting Patella Reflex—blocking progress in the workplace all the time. At a small television news service where he was a sales administrator, Joseph noticed that all the client records were kept by hand. He asked the president of the company for permission to install a computerized database that would automatically track contract renewals, licensing fees, and the like.

"Joseph, if that database goes down, what happens to all of our client information? In this business, our client information is all we have. I'm not entrusting that to any computer unless you can absolutely guarantee that it's going to be one hundred percent operative, one hundred percent of the time."

It's clear enough that Joseph's boss thought that he listened to Joseph's proposal. His response was logical; it followed from what Joseph asked for. But the response also clearly came through a filter: Joseph's boss believed that computers were unreliable, or perhaps mysterious and subject to all manner of calamity. The boss's filter had installed itself automatically—he didn't need to do anything, and there it was.

When we listen through a filter, we evaluate the content of the person's message by what's hiding in the filter, as happened to Joseph's boss. We can't hover above the comment and receive the kind of insights that will get us an *aha* or a *wow*. We just fall into the black hole of that issue—waiting for our Patella Reflex to be struck.

Although Joseph eventually did convince his boss to install the database (we're happy to report that the company's renewal rates improved as a direct result), Joseph eventually left the company feeling underutilized and underappreciated, and was secretly happy when the company's corporate parent put it up for sale. "If my boss had just listened to me," he said, "maybe I could have made an impact there." Joseph speaks for millions of working Americans. According to several recent surveys, one of employees' chief gripes about their bosses is that they don't listen.[3]

If we listen normally, we have two choices. Either we: (a) pretend to listen but really focus on our thoughts and then miss the person's message (shiny objects), or (b) we listen through a filter and get sucked into the black hole of evaluating the issue *we're* hearing about (Patella Reflex). Without a different kind of listening, we'll never get people through the "see" stage. Coaches listen in a way that produces those magic words—*duh, aha, wow,* and *shazam.*

How Coaches Listen

One well-known business coach we interviewed helped turn around a major division of a *Fortune* 500 corporation. We asked him how he did it. Without a second of hesitation, he said: "I just listened until they told me who they were." No, this person isn't a crystal-rubbing tree-hugger. And no, this isn't a veiled reference to new age spirituality.

Vocabulary time. We'll call what this coach did "listening *for*,"[4] and we'll call the everyday kind "listening *to*."

When Paul, the board member and co-owner of the troubled company we talked about in the beginning of this chapter, told us that he wanted dirt on the conspirators, he didn't know it, but one of the other board members was listening *to* him. He came over to us later and wanted to gossip about Paul's instruction for us to go find a conspiracy in the company. "It just made me so f——ing mad," he said. This board member had listened to Paul's gripes, and had been sucked into the black hole of hunting for conspirators rather than doing what was best for the company. His filter betrayed him.

What made us different is that we listened *for* the person's motivation. It was clear that his motivation was revenge, and that wasn't why we were there. This gave us the insight to wring out a *duh*. To listen for the person's motivation, practice the steps in the following section.

Lube, Oil, and Filter

Step One: Gain Awareness of Your Filters

The first step to listening like a coach may be the simplest. And yet it's the step manager-coaches in the making need to repeat over and over. It simply entails becoming aware of what's happening when we try to listen.

It's a hard step. We have to recognize that we all—including you and me—listen through interpretive filters we previously did not know were there.

Filters are like the air we breathe—we don't know it's there until it's brought to our attention. Like anything that's worthwhile, it takes a certain amount of work even to start seeing our filters. Some filters are so old, so deeply ingrained, and so firmly in place that even when we're looking for them, we won't recognize them. That's okay.

Read over the following statements and notice how you respond when the words enter your brain:

1. Employees are lazy.
2. DMV workers are incompetent.
3. Most managers are just out for their own success.

If you noticed yourself judging the statements as right or wrong, or thinking of examples to prove or disprove the statement, take a moment and introduce yourself to one of your filters.

In this first step toward listening like a coach, we notice—or "see"— how our filters guide our response when we're speaking with others. Notice again how many different filters we have, and how seamlessly they change to fit every situation.

Our minds are so advanced at using filters to make judgments that we think those judgments are actually cold, hard facts. "Bill *is* a slacker," we might say, without realizing that the statement is the result of a filter.

"But there's evidence! Bill hasn't shown up for work, and hasn't produced a thing. He *is* lazy. He *is* a slacker."

The filter's at work again. Bill is just Bill. Evaluations aren't right or wrong, they're just evaluations that pop out of the filter. Bill isn't at work right now—true. Bill is lazy—evaluation from a filter.

A great example of a filter at work comes to us from one of the "Big Five" accounting firms. One of the partners often argued against promoting what he called "social butterflies," because, he said, "they never get any work done."

While this partner wasn't completely responsible for promotional decisions, his opinion carried a lot of weight—until a meeting a year ago to discuss promotions. A recent college graduate was being considered for an early promotion to "senior associate."

"No way," the partner said. "A social butterfly. All she does is talk, talk, talk." That was the end of it.

Until another partner noted that her billable hours were higher than anyone else's. And yet another partner said that the clients have reported how much value she added. And another partner said that she is at work before everyone else and that her work is better than that of many of the MBAs.

And then the kicker: another partner asked why "Scrooge" (as he was known from that day forward) was always hard on people who developed friendships with clients and coworkers. "We want to promote people like this woman, because they can grow the business," this other partner snapped. "But you only want to promote people with no social skills—people like you." If influence were visible, "Scrooge" would have seen his dripping away through the floor—all because his filter prevented him from seeing the value in one of his employees.

Take some time to just notice how your filters kick in, evaluate issues, and then swap themselves out for other filters when the topic changes. Everybody has them, but few people are aware of them. This first step can be frustrating, but it will give you an advantage over people who don't know they have filters.

Step Two: Consciously Change Filters

The most famous American feud, between the Hatfields and the McCoys, lasted for generations and killed dozens of people. By the time it ended, no one could remember why it started. By then it didn't matter: everyone involved had a filter firmly in place that guided everything they heard and said about everyone else. Everyone was "right" (filters make people feel right), including all the people who were dead.

If only someone would have had the insight and the spine to change filters, the bloody feud might have ended before everyone was sucked into the same black hole. Learning to consciously change filters prepares you to listen like a coach—and might just keep you out of duels.

In this second step, when you catch a glimpse of a filter, try to swap it out for another one.

Returning to the example of Bill the slacker, there are many other ways of thinking about the same person. Bill might be an extremely hard-working person, but he has trouble setting priorities. Or he might have a poor work/life balance, so that other issues in his life are crowding out his work performance. Each of these interpretations falls out of a different filter—just as different filters for a camera give very different versions of the same picture.

Step Three: Go Deep

The first two steps prepare you to listen without immediately getting sucked into the content of an issue with judgments and evaluations. As a manager-coach, you're now ready to experience some of the magic of coaching.

The technique we're about to show you, which is part of active listening,[5] and counseling, stands on its own as a coaching device.

For this next step, plan a time to talk with one of your employees when you won't be interrupted by phone calls or emergencies. Even five minutes is enough, but it has to be uninterrupted time.

The first part of "going deep" is to re-establish the safe coaching environment. We call this first part "getting in with" the person—it's the process of renewing your connection to his or her hopes, dreams, and values. "Getting in with" the person you're coaching is more a matter of really caring about the person than using specific words. If you seem rushed, or are eager to check your e-mail, you won't "get in with" the person.

Once "in," and you will know you're in by their nonverbals (leaning forward, more at ease), test the environment by asking the person a question about something important to him or her, such as "What do you like about your job?" When the person responds, listen for the one word that is most important. If she says: "I really enjoy the constant change in responsibilities," perhaps it's the word "constant," or "change," or "responsibilities."

Take this key word and repeat it back, in the form of a question. If you pick "change," you might ask "What about change is so important to you?" We call this "clicking," just as you would "click" on a word in a Web page. Usually, this links you to a page that gives you richer information about that word. When you "click" on one of the person's words, you get deeper—and closer to the person's Core Values. To take the technique a step further, add the nonverbal communication consistent with really listening—leaning forward, paying close attention, making eye contact, and so on. When you mix following up on what the person says with a question and adding these nonverbals, we call it "double clicking."

Listen and watch for their expression carefully to be certain that they are not simply saying what you want to hear. You must realize, as a manager-coach, that if they are "snowing" you, then you have failed to establish the all-important safe environment. You must return to that level and "get in with" them for real. Sometimes, in difficult cases, you must look them straight in the eye and ask them directly, "What can I do to establish a stronger rapport between us?" They need to know—really know—that you are serious about your relationship with them. You are there to serve them. This is a case where faking it won't make it; they will see right through you.

Once you have tested the environment with the important question, and you are sure that you are "in" with them, ask them what they want to take away from the coaching session.

Double "click" on their responses, allowing them to free associate to a degree. But if they are blaming others or circumstances, do not go down that pathway. It is both typical and predictable that people go this direction and like to take others with them. Don't do it—you will lose all effectiveness as a coach if you get suckered into this direction.

A great coach never gives up on people's potential (even when *they* have) by agreeing that they are a victim of someone or something. At some point, the outflow from them might falter. This is okay. It just means that they are unsure of their safety. Ask their permission to go further. Let them know that it is safe to talk candidly with you.

After they have said what they have to say, repeat back to them what you heard. Verify that what you are repeating is what they meant. Give them the opportunity to correct anything that you may have misunderstood or misinterpreted. Do this until they agree that you are saying it correctly. Be careful not to change their wording or put it into "your own words." Also, be very careful not to put words into their mouth or trap them in any way. This is a very delicate part of coaching, and they must be allowed and encouraged to say what doesn't work about their job without being criticized or you will lose their trust and respect.

After this step in coaching, be sure to validate their point of view. You may not agree with it, but it is their point of view, and it is at the heart of why you are having this conversation with them. Thank them for being honest with you.

Next, ask them if you have heard and understood everything that they said to you. Again, it is not necessary to them that you agree, but it is necessary, even vital, to them that you heard and understood.

Our metaphor for this part of the coaching process is a treasure hunt. Imagine that whatever the person says is covering up the real gold in their communication to you. It's obvious that you need to have that person trust you so that they will allow you to get to the treasure—the real thing that they are trying to say. This is why you have to "get in with" this person. They must trust that you are really listening to them.

Use this process to go deeper and deeper with them until you are clear that you are at the root of their concern. You will know you are there when the issue becomes simple and clear to them. Often, they will physically shift their body position and a look of relief will cross their face. Often, they will state the obvious solution to their concern or issue in a very clear manner—if they don't, say the obvious for them and watch for their response. You might get a *duh*, *aha*, or a *wow*.

Once you have established a safe environment, the process itself goes very quickly, usually less than five minutes. At the end of the session—if you've gone deep on enough words—you will have uncovered the treasure and you'll understand more about this person's motivations and values than if you've spent a year as her friend. It really is that effective.

What happens if you pick the wrong word, one that doesn't take you deeper? You'll get an odd look, which is a signal that you should pick a different word and try again.

Here's the payoff: you'll deeply explore this person's real career interests and passions, without getting sucked into agreeing or disagreeing, which is the pull of most filters.

Step Four: Listen "For" Their Core Values, Deep Motivations, and Unrealized Potential

As you're "going deep" in discussion, listen *for* the things that make this person unique—and that they haven't admitted to themselves. This is different than listening *to* what they say—which either allows our minds to wander in reaction to their statements (Patella Reflex), or exit to a completely different topic (shiny objects).

Core values are one of the most important topics for manager-coaches. People usually won't use this title, but during a "go deep" discussion, they'll usually tell you what's important to them. In many cases, they'll tell you something that they haven't admitted to themselves.

Coauthor John King has a client who recently sold a consulting business for a large sum of money. Part of the sale included a non-compete agreement between his client and the buyer. For the first time in this person's life, he not only didn't have to work, but was contractually barred from working—at least in the one field he knew best.

In discussions with John, the client lamented that he couldn't work in consulting anymore. At times, he griped that he had lost his identity. But by "going deep" through "double clicking" and listening for Core Values, John realized that his client's dedication was to impacting the world, not to consulting. John pointed out this insight to the client, who, at first, argued that John wasn't hearing him. "I was born to consult," he fired back.

This is the signal to a coach that it's time to go deep again. "What about consulting is so important to you?" John asked, keying in on the vibrant word that was so important to his client and "double clicking" on it.

"I come and go on my terms," was his answer.

"So you're dedicated to living your life on your terms?" John asked.

"Well, no," he said, realizing that saying "yes" would make him seem shallow.

"So what about consulting is so important?" John asked again.

"I suppose it's that I can make a difference in a short period of time," he answered.

"So is your dedication to making a difference, and consulting your vehicle for doing this?" John asked.

"I suppose it is," he said thoughtfully, followed by "hmmm."

In the world of coaching, *hmmm* is sometimes a synonym for *aha*.

When you hear something that you think is a Core Value or deep motivation for the person, interrupt the "going deep" process and point out your observation. For example, if the person says "I really love challenge," you might say: "It sounds as though you're a highly ambitious person." If you've really been listening "for" their values and motivations, most of the time the response will be "yes!" If it's something the person hasn't admitted to themselves, you might even get an *aha* or a *wow*.

When you hear something about the person's potential, you've struck gold. But be careful—unrealized potential is the most powerful force in nature. When the potential energy in a nuclear bomb is released, a city can be vaporized in a millisecond. When a person's potential is realized, he or she can literally become a different person.

In the case of John's client, he used that insight to find a new way of making a difference that didn't involve consulting. He had the best of all possible worlds—the money from selling a successful enterprise and the insight that his Core Values had left him with many more things yet to do.

Champions from all fields report that there was a single moment when someone else "saw" their Core Values. In that moment, they "saw" themselves differently, and a new world of opportunity appeared before them.

In coaching thousands of managers, executives, and entrepreneurs, we've noticed that many will not want to hear about their potential or their Core Values. For them, a filter will kick in that tells them they really don't have much potential, or that their potential is too hard to develop.

John recently coached a manager of a large health care organization. After "going deep" in several conversations, she discussed her own belief that the company had to become responsive to change, and that key employees had to start feeling valued. The potential John saw was that she truly cared for each and every employee, even those that didn't work for her. She had the potential to grow into a great corporate leader with the ability to rally support at all levels of the company. When he told her this, she said, "Oh, that'll never happen" and moved on. John had to return to the topic several times before she finally heard him. When she did, she sat back in her chair, her eyes wide with excitement and surprise. Finally a long *wow* filled the room.

She had "seen" a glimpse of her potential and her world had changed. She is now the "heir apparent" in this organization, and will likely rise to become its next president. This is the power of "seeing" potential.

Step Five: Listen "For" Gaps Between Personal Vision and Action

When you hear the person's vision for their job and career, it will sound idyllic. For 90 percent of people, it will be totally detached from what they do every day.

Most managers will say that they want their people empowered, to think of new and valuable ideas. Yet their actions betray this desire. We are forced to agree with Ross Perot, who recently said: "There are guys all over American industry that spent thirty years eating dirt. They finally got in a position of responsibility and they see their role in life is to make everybody eat dirt that works for them."[6]

We coached the president of a chemical company, who said that his goal was to return to profitability. Yet every chance he got, he seemed to take actions that ensured his company would *never* be profitable—like when he stopped the development of a product that was almost finished because he thought a second product—that was barely off computer simulations—could make money. Going down this path meant he'd have to take out more corporate debt.

When that product was almost finished, he switched to a third product. John pointed out the difference between what he said he wanted to do, and what his actions were achieving.

The person uttered one of our favorite words: *duh*, meaning that he "saw" something missing: follow-through on his plans.

Yet before getting to the *duh*, he explained, in all the technical jargon his dual-masters'-degree mind could muster, why the actions he was taking were correct. His filter prevented him from admitting he was trotting down a path that led to a sheer cliff.

This is where a manager-coach has to be *very* careful about their own filters. Many manager-coaches will respond to the objections by agreeing or disagreeing with them—the Patella Reflex—instead of going deep, listening *for* Core Values, deep motivations, potential, and gaps.

We recently worked with an executive whose people nicked him "Deadline Doug." His assistant warned him about the title, but the joke was lost on him. He adopted it as his nickname, often telling his direct reports "Just give me deadlines—I'm Deadline Doug, remember?"

Doug wanted the benefits of being a manager-coach, so he contracted with us to help. We sat through a meeting with him, and we spotted his patella reflex right away. "I have an idea," one of his people said.

"When can it be done?" he responded, without even knowing what the idea was.

"Ah . . . that depends on what part of it you like," she responded, obviously not liking the direction Doug was taking this.

"Whichever part can be done right away, 'cause we need to get results."

"I can implement a small part right away, say by next Friday."

"Friday's too long. How about next Wednesday?" A smile began to cross his face.

The meeting continued. "I guess," she said, her unhappiness visible to everyone in the room except Doug.

"Then let's go get it done!" Doug stood up, signaling the meeting was over.

As she left, Doug turned to us and said, "See how I added value?" We pointed out that the value he added was telling an employee to implement part of an idea he hadn't heard, against her better judgment.

Eventually, we got a *duh*. He was then ready to listen like a coach.

There's an old motto we've heard from several coaches: "A coach reminds a person of who he is, even when he forgets." If you use this as your motto in listening, you'll listen like a coach.

In the case of the chemicals executive, John had to remind him over a dozen times that he was dedicated to making his company profitable. The problem was that when a sexy new idea came along, it got his attention. John had to remind him of his commitments and force him to choose—either follow through on his stated goals or reset those goals. But either way, he had to stop griping about his lack of solvency, because he was responsible for 100 percent of it.

When the manager-coach is actually listening, the people around her will tell her "who they truly are." In other words, they'll trust her with their vision of how great their jobs can be. They'll tell her all about how much of an impact they want to have. Coaches recognize that when people do this, they're actually putting a new, and more effective, filter in place. And they're doing it perhaps for the first time.

As a rule, we understand much of the world backwards. We think that what we say influences people, moves projects forward, or gets things done. Instead, it's actually how we listen that has the greater influence. Notice how people seem to become just the way their reputations suggest they are. It's because that's what people around them expect, and it's what those people are "listening for."

It stands to reason, then, that when we control how we listen, we can use those strong listening skills to influence the people around us. Coaches use the way they listen to give the people around them the power to achieve, to produce, to accomplish. When coaches listen for people to produce outstanding results, that's precisely what happens. People often say that "you get what you pay for." Carpenters say "you get what you measure for." What coaches understand, and what they rely on as a large part of their arsenal, is that you get what you listen for.

chapter three

"Seeing" a World-Class Culture

Coauthor Dave Logan had a truly bizarre experience when he consulted for a large agency of the federal government in Washington D.C. When he first got to his hotel room and tried to unwind by flipping channels in front of the TV, there was nothing but static on all the channels—except the one cable channel that was running a marathon of *The X-Files*. He had to laugh at it—sitting here in the nation's capital and the only thing that comes on television is a show about fictional secrets and cover-ups of the government.

"If that was amusing, the next day was downright frustrating," he bemoaned. He spent eight hours talking about leadership to people who looked at him with what coauthor John King calls the "thousand-yard stare"—a glassy-eyed stare from someone who's been so emotionally damaged by battlefield combat that the only solution is to hook them up to a lithium drip.

On the flight back, Dave sat next to a man who was reading a book with a picture of someone holding an automatic weapon on the dust jacket. Curious, he looked closer and saw it was a book about conspiracy theories involving the same government agency for which he had just finished consulting. At first he giggled inside, but the irony was too great. "I ended up laughing so hard that Pepsi came out my nose," he joked.

Dave got the man's attention, unfortunately. The guy proceeded to tell him how this agency was going to carry out an elaborate plan to form one world government in which they would have all the power. Black helicopters, UN soldiers, UFOs—they were all there, like another episode of *The X-Files*. "These people?" Dave opened his big mouth, knowing he'd regret it, but trying to forget the Pepsi incident. "They're not capable of planning a conspiracy even if they wanted to. Trust me, they have a hard enough time planning the day."

We have nothing against people with different beliefs, and we do think that our government performs many positive services and employs mostly capable, service-minded people. But if we're honest, we have to admit that some parts of the government are not well run.

Take the DMV. In a world where you can bank, pay bills, shop, even date electronically without stepping out your front door, the simple task of renewing a driver's license involves losing a day's work waiting in a line stretching out to the parking lot. And when the line gets longer, employees decide it's a good time to take breaks. At least this has been our experience—and the experience of everyone we seem to talk to.

Yet there are plenty of talented, competent people in the DMV. How is it possible? It's our contention that competence and incompetence are primarily a result of the kind of culture in an organization.

Louis Koster is the president of Strategic Business Developments, a consulting firm focusing on transformational coaching for companies. As a physician, he spent years with Doctors Without Borders (a group that recently won the Nobel Peace Prize) in troubled parts of the world, such as Bosnia. In reflecting on his Core Values, he "saw" that his real dedication was to peace, so he left the practice of medicine and started a consulting organization.

His consulting team donates a significant part of its time promoting peace in many of the places Dr. Koster used to operate on the wounded. He tells one story about bringing two cultures together—showing how culture drives individual performance.

After the fall of communism in Romania, several outside experts came in to teach people different skills, such as modern accounting methods and "how to become a leader."

"The problem is that leadership doesn't happen in isolation," Dr. Koster noted to us in a recent interview with him. "If a person acted like a leader in communist Romania, he'd get killed. This is a culture where one in three was a member of the secret police. It's not a place where you wanted to get noticed." It's also not a place where people will tend to put Generally Accepted Accounting Principles ahead of staying alive.

Even after the fall of communism, this culture persists in the country. Dr. Koster's team consulted to a group of medical professionals that included both general practitioners and university professors (who determined national policy rather autocratically). He says, "The professors thought the practitioners were dim-witted, and the practitioners thought the professors were too 'ivory tower.' To make it worse, the university system controlled most of the resources and made all of the decisions, while the practitioners were the ones treating Romania's citizens and who had practical knowledge. This cultural rift was costing everyone dearly."

Through a process of working with both groups, Dr. Koster's team helped everyone involved to "see" why the culture was the way it was, and that it was a system everyone had inherited. Once they "saw" the culture for what it was, and that it was a by-product of decades of tyranny in the country, they were able to change it. Together, these two groups started aligning their efforts, and the result is "truly historic," Dr. Koster reports. "It's the first time they're working together for the betterment of healthcare throughout Romania."

As we'll see, knowledge in how culture drives performance is essential for manager-coaches.

What Academics Have Long Known

Back in 1921, Edward Sapir and Benjamin Whorf started a revolution in several academic fields by arguing that language and culture are inseparable. This idea became known as the "Sapir-Whorf" hypothesis.[1] It has been seen in so many research studies that most leading psychologists and communication experts believe it with the same strength they believe the world is round.

Martin Heidegger extended the Sapir-Whorf hypothesis by saying, "Man acts as though *he* were the shaper and master of language, while in fact *language* remains the master of man."[2]

The well-known scholar Kenneth Burke would argue that the words we use not only describe environment, they create environment. He wrote:

"Even if a given terminology is a *reflection* of reality, but by its very nature as a terminology it must be a *selection* of reality; and to this extent it must function also as a *deflection* of reality."[3]

In our consulting, we often come across people who describe normal events, stuff that goes on every day, as "problems." Some will even go so far as to call these everyday occurrences "crises." Managers using these words seldom realize that their vocabulary deeply concerns, even panics, many employees. If an angry customer's phone call is a "crisis" (because he might get the customer service department in trouble), it's impossible to also think of his call as an "opportunity." It's *either* a crisis *or* an opportunity. It can't be both at the same time. The selection of the word "crisis" simultaneously *reflects* a reality of panic and problems, while it *deflects* a reality of opportunity and the chance to change for the better.

Dale Smalley, a Practice Leader in Management and Organizational Development at Philip Morris, recently reminded us of the power of words. In a prior job, Dale worked with Holiday Inn as Director of Management and Systems Development. Senior managers at the hotel chain were trying to distinguish outstanding performance from merely adequate performance. They asked Dale to come up with a word that would highlight the desired behavior.

After thinking about it, discussing the issue with people, and doing some research, Dale proposed the word "commendable." The management was thrilled. Dale reports: "Soon 'commendable' was everywhere. It really altered the way people thought about their jobs."

But there's a dark side to the simple uses of words. "Immature people, according to experts, use a narrow range of words to describe what they see. This limits their ability to be flexible," Dale mentioned to us. "So naming things is important, but it shouldn't be overdone. You want to empower people. A single word that explains everything disempowers them."

"I'm concerned about phrases like 'going forward,' which inexperienced managers sometimes use over and over without thinking of other ways to look at it," he continued. It reminded us of what Burke said: as you label a situation, so you will respond to it. Label it a crisis, and you'll respond as if it's a crisis. Label it an opportunity and everything changes.

We used the idea that language and culture are inseparable as our starting point and then studied over two dozen corporate cultures. We expected to find about two dozen types of cultures and as many uses of language. To our surprise, we noticed that five clear categories emerged. Each category represents a culture, held together by the common use of words.

In fact, each culture had its own "language police." Anyone who didn't use language consistent with the culture was ostracized or taken out and shot, figuratively speaking. We actually found people with the audacity to correct other people's phrasing.

At one troubled company, a manager stormed out of his office after getting a disturbing call from a customer. "Incoming!" he yelled, as if bombs were about to obliterate the building.

Another manager at his level, newly hired in the company, watched him storm past. This new manager asked one of the tenured employees why everything was seen as an attack. "Because that's the way it is," was his quick answer. The culture was so powerful that long-time employees thought it was real and that there was no other way to look at it.

The same day, the tenured employee pulled the new manager aside and busted him for a cultural violation. "Take down the pictures of your Hawaii vacation," he said. "We need to focus on the incoming jobs and nothing can distract us." Only then did the new manager realize he was the only person to have anything personal in his office. He quickly took down his pictures. The culture had recruited another member.

This almost invisible "correcting" perpetuates the dominant culture and makes change almost impossible. This insight answered a question that many have asked: why doesn't somebody fix the DMV? The answer is that the minute anyone tried, the "language police" would get everyone to use the old language—and remember that language determines action. The "language police" would make sure the old culture lived on.

So why is this important? And what does it have to do with coaching?

If a manager-coach can help people to "see" a culture that's superior to the culture that exists all around them, they will have taken the first steps to changing the culture. From our research, culture is the single biggest determinant of an organization's success or failure.

Five Cultures at Work

Without intending to portray any one of these cultures in a negative way, we chose to use terms that illustrate the distinctiveness of each. The names describe the level of employee satisfaction as much as the effectiveness of that culture's communication. The ineffective cultures have dramatically decreased productivity and increased employee turnover. To put it bluntly, these cultures cost everyone—the employees, the customers, the managers, and anyone connected with the organization.

Here they are:

The Five Cultures		
Name of Culture/ Effectiveness	*Key Theme/ Metaphor of Culture*	*Employees' Connections with Each Other*
Vital	"Life Is Great"	Teamwork
Important	"We're Great"	Partnership
Useful	"I'm Great"	Personal
Ineffective	"I'm a Victim"	Separate
Undermining	"Life Sucks"	Alienated

The "Undermining" Culture

Let's go back to the government agency at the center of those conspiracy theories. During our time with the organization, virtually no work was produced. People spent their time in meetings discussing which steps to plan to take. Which led to more meetings where people planned again. So when did the work get done? It didn't.

It is no exaggeration to say that people spent all day standing outside their offices drinking coffee and gossiping about how budget cuts would negatively affect their lives. In all their gossip, not once did we hear any mention about how budget cuts might affect their constituencies.

In one-on-one interviews we found that for them this was just "life as usual" in the working world. Nobody really cared about the customer, because things were so bad on the inside.

So why didn't a good manager fix the problem? Several in our research tried. But they all emphasized personal change, not cultural change. Dale Smalley from Philip Morris reminds us of the limitation of this approach. "In clinical family practice, many experts think you can't just 'fix' one person. If there's abuse or addiction, the whole family culture supports it, probably without knowing it. The 'fixed' person might be 'unfixed' by the people around them." This is the power of culture.

The three "undermining" cultures we found had these things in common:

- Low morale
- A deep alienation from people in the culture
- Virtually no "team spirit"
- A bitter mindset
- A tendency to react negatively to people who appeared to have a more positive outlook

The common theme among "undermining" cultures is that life, by nature, is out to get people. Anyone who bucked this "obvious" fact was treated like a troublemaker. One of the new guys at this government agency was openly mocked as "positive-thinking boy." Naturally, those mocking him had been there a while. These people truly believed that "life sucks." And while this point of view is held to be the truth by the employees at this agency, sadly, the attitude of the employees is keenly felt by the customers of such "undermining" cultures and spreads all over them when they do business.

So what do you do if you work in an undermining culture? There are steps to improving the environment, as we'll see later in this chapter.

The "Ineffective" Culture

The difference between cultures that are "undermining" and cultures that are "ineffective" is that people expressed a personal theme of victimization in the latter. Rather than thinking "life sucks" in general, they believe it just sucks for them. They feel special and unique about being the victims and martyrs of life. In "ineffective" cultures, life is fine—just not where these folks work. During our research, we observed seven companies with ineffective cultures.

One team, for example, in the HR department for a health services provider spent 45 minutes out of an hour-long meeting explaining how upper management accepted none of their recent recommendations. Two people dominated the meeting, as the others sat there demoralized. One person kept repeating, "They don't appreciate us," while the other said, over and over, "We're not taken seriously." There was an overriding sense of imposed impotence—management was not giving them what they needed to work effectively. The fact is, management was bending over backwards to work with this team.

In the seven cultures like this, we noticed these things in common:

- Low morale
- A deep sense of powerlessness in the culture
- Virtually no "team spirit"
- Consistent utterance of victimization themes
- A tendency to resign from high-profile assignments

The "Useful" Culture

There is a marked difference between the next three cultures and the ones we categorized as "undermining" and "ineffective"—these cultures were productive and much more positive.

The predominating theme of "useful" cultures is one of personal competence: "Aren't I great!" An example of this came in a technical support team meeting in which one person after another reported solving intricate, technical problems. Although there was a general experience of personal accomplishment, there was no broadly shared sense of vision or teamwork. No one seemed to see any connection, any "big picture" in what they did. Each individual was focused on his or her own work without seeing how it related to the rest of the team.

"Useful" cultures seem especially prevalent in sales organizations, where one's ability to push goods or services not only makes money for the company, but makes their commission, as well.

Yet the dark side to "useful" cultures is that the old adage "no man is an island" doesn't seem to apply. In these cultures, every person is an island. Each person's discussion is oriented around his or her greatness, his or her competence, his or her achievements, all on a personal level. There is no sense of partnership.

Among the five "useful" cultures, we noticed these things in common:

- Fluctuating levels of morale, based upon individual accomplishments
- A sense of personal accomplishment in the culture
- Low "team spirit"
- A focus on solving problems
- An emphasis on the details of people's job descriptions, rather than on team goals
- Low levels of trust for coworkers

The "Important" Culture

Unlike "useful" cultures, which see competence as personal, the theme of "important" cultures is *group* competence. The morale—and hence, the customer service—was much higher in these cultures. There was a sense of "partnership" and "teamwork" in the three "important" cultures we researched.

On the downside, we also noticed an "us-them" attitude mixed with an "aren't we great!" spirit. They accomplished great things, and so they were great from a certain perspective. But there was a highly competitive attitude. Other groups were seen as less competent, even as less moral. "Our team" was simply superior in every way—and had a greater right to exist.

We saw a perfect example of this competitive theme in a health care provider. The team's communication focused on how much more successful they were than the medical center affiliated with the university across town.

In the three "important" cultures, we found these things in common:

- High morale
- A sense of superiority in the culture
- High team spirit
- A focus on accomplishment
- A clear team vision
- A theme of "our" competence and superiority compared to "theirs" (usually, one other group or organization)

The "Vital" Culture

This is where we would like to see every culture—whether in non-profit or for-profit organizations. The "vital" cultures have all the competence and team spirit of the "important" cultures, minus the "us-them" focus. In "vital" cultures, there is no *other* group. The team vision includes everyone. We were fortunate to find two "vital" cultures in our research—one in biotechnology and the other in an entrepreneurial, start-up venture.

At a biotechnology department meeting, several people expressed how the company's products are extending the length and quality of people's lives. The focus is on people in general, not on an in-group. In one-on-one conversations with people in "vital" cultures, we found that this sense of mission to improve the quality of life for all people was genuine.

They had these things in common:

- High morale
- A strong sense of mission in the culture
- High team spirit
- A focus on impacting the world in a positive way
- Other companies/departments might be adversarial, but we never observed the "us-them" split—commonly, they are regarded as "partners" in accomplishing "the mission"

The Coaching Revolution Comes Home

The purpose of this book is to empower managers to become manager-coaches. Part of the revolution that's going on in business today is that employees are simply not tolerating bad places to work. It's vital, then, that managers in the lower-level cultures raise the standard and boost performance. In essence, it's the job of the manager to raise the culture in the department. But how can he or she do this?

Remember the "ineffective" culture at the health care provider? We showed them the five cultures model, and they were ecstatic about what the model helped them "see"—the potential of becoming vital. But then when we pointed out where they were on the chart, they quickly deflated. Once they pulled themselves together they made a collective agreement to boost their communication to the "important" level.

This is the key step for manager-coaches. You have to show people their potential to rise on the cultural ladder—and yet show them the truth about their current culture. When they "see" their potential—and the gaps—they will have taken the first steps to becoming a world-class team.

After collecting qualitative and quantitative data during our six-month intervention, they've shown marked signs of improvement. They actually shifted their culture—but only to the "useful" level.

We're still working with this group and throughout our training and executive coaching sessions, we are seeing signs of an "important" culture. The most effective tool has been to point out where they are culturally and to remind them of their commitment to elevate their culture.

Improved Cultures Through Coaching

Two years ago, a Social Security Administration office in the Seattle region began to realize they had a crisis in the making. Employees were unhappy, morale was low, customer service was down, and the manager of a key division sought to find a solution. He turned to Jackie Nagel, the long-time business coach mentioned in Chapter 1. Jackie worked with the manager and then with the employees, using training and individualized coaching sessions to probe into individual issues.

As Jackie tells the story, her main service was to "listen until people learn who they really are," as discussed in the last chapter. Once they came to understand and embrace their unique combination of skills, interests, and values, they were in a much better position to develop themselves inside their jobs. Some went back to school. Others applied for management jobs. Most stayed with the Social Security Administration and contributed much more after the coaching than they had before. As a result of their heightened understanding of themselves and their coworkers, their ability to work toward common goals increased. The culture improved, the morale rose, and the productivity level of almost every person soared.

In fact, this Social Security office did something almost unheard of in government: it extended its hours because the employees wanted to better service their customers. Their culture rose from "ineffective" to "important" through coaching.

As manager-coaches, this is where you'll begin. Where is your team on the five cultures chart? Where would you like it to be? We suggest talking with people about it, getting their perspective through the "go deep" method mentioned in Chapter 2. Help them to "see" where they are and where they can go. If you hear an *aha*, you're done with the first step. Read on to move ahead.

chapter four

The Spin and the Trash Bag

Carlos became known around his office as "Dr. No," much to his frustration. He couldn't understand why. Wasn't he the same cool guy? He used to be a hip, rock-n-roll DJ in college. Something changed when he rose into management. Work wasn't fun anymore. He had to hire people, fire people, and listen to and screen their ludicrous ideas before taking them to his boss, George, the Senior VP of media marketing.

Carlos had a lot to complain about—mainly about the people under him, who, he felt, had disappointed him. On a typical afternoon, he would catch Larry falling asleep in his office, Josh playing Solitaire on his computer, Brett, Kevin, and Maria gossiping by the water cooler. He didn't know what Mike did behind his closed office door all day, but it certainly didn't resemble the projects he asked Mike to do. In fact, Brett, Kevin, and Maria had a pet name for Mike—"Mushroom"—because he liked to be alone in the dark. And then there was Richard. Richard was just weird. He dressed weird. He taped weird things to his door, like pictures of Klingons. He even claimed he could speak Klingon.

Sometimes Carlos, even though he was the manager, would throw up his hands and join in staff-level gossip with Maria, Brett, and Kevin. At least they were people he could talk to. And they never brought up Klingons, unless they were laughing at Richard.

What Carlos didn't realize was that his own constant complaining spread all over the office, like the stench of trash. No wonder the staff was afraid to tell him any of their wild ideas. Carlos would just "piss all over it," in their words.

Then the trouble hit. The company lost 9 percent of market share in one quarter. Corporate officers picked up scalpels in search of fat to trim. Most agreed that Carlos's staff needed to be on the short list. In a board meeting, they fired zingers at Carlos's boss, George: "Nobody knows what your people do in there. They're just mushrooms and Klingons."

After the meeting, George yanked Carlos into his office. "Everyone's job is on the line, including mine. We need to justify our existence, every one of us."

It was a difficult time for everyone on the staff. While they didn't know it, every one of their jobs was vitally and immediately dependent upon Carlos throwing out his trash. His mental trash, that is.

The Problem

Many people are remarkable in their perseverance. They try the same approach over, and over, and over. It never works, but this doesn't discourage them. They'll just try again. This pattern is so ineffective and common that it's been studied in depth by some of the most famous psychologists in history. Jacques Lacan called this tendency "repetition compulsion."[1]

Yogi Berra called this activity "the vicious circus." We call it "the spin."

The spin is a devious problem because people don't know they're doing the same thing over and over. Each time, the situation is just different enough to make them think they're responding in a new way. They might even think they're learning and growing.

According to many psychologists, people can become addicted to the spin just as they can become addicted to the overuse of tobacco or alcohol. In every addiction, the substance of the addiction is an attempt to numb, or run from, mental pain.

Jay Malone is spinning. As a manager in a major nonprofit organization, he tried to build a feeling of camaraderie by being "one of the guys." He went so far as to curse whenever he could, just so people wouldn't think he was stuffy. They didn't. One of his direct reports, a religious person, became so frustrated that he asked Jay to stop. Jay did stop—until the situation at work became stressful around budgeting time for the next year.

Jay felt that he needed to get everyone's support. He would never admit this to anyone else, but he thought if he could boost his department's budget, he'd be in line for a promotion. It was all riding on his ability to get his people to work together and justify a bigger piece of the nonprofit's pie.

At the start of a meeting with his staff, Jay felt the pressure of wanting to be "one of the guys." So, without even thinking it through, he told an especially off-color joke involving sex. After the punch line, when nervous laughter filled the room, the same person who had asked Jay to stop the offensive language got up, left the room, and walked straight to the HR director's office, and lodged a formal complaint. Jay was warned in writing that his behavior was unacceptable and was never promoted again.

Jay exhibited the fundamental error of using the same approach, over and over, even when it's not working. Jay was the son of a preacher, and all through his childhood, he always thought that people felt he was better than they—more moral, more in control. Inwardly, he felt out of control. His childhood was lonely. Even as an adult, Jay felt separate from people—even when they didn't know anything about his father.

This mental pain became so extreme that Jay would get nervous before every meeting. He'd feel his underarms perspiring and his heart pounding loudly. The only way he knew to drive the uncomfortable feeling away was to joke with people.

So every time Jay would get that uncomfortable feeling, he'd compensate with his addiction—a crass joke or a curse—and he was on his way into the spin. Jay didn't realize it, but he was an addict.

Most people do not recognize when they are in the spin without outside help. Jay's motto—which he believed he was living up to—was "every day, in every way, I'm becoming better and better." However, the sad truth was, every day and in every way, Jay remained exactly the same.

People like Jay need support—an objective coach who points out ineffective behavior and works with them to ensure that they don't circle around and around in the spin, as Jay did.

Harold Geneen, the person who built ITT into the first conglomerate, argued strongly that people who command others often haven't dealt effectively with their own insecurities—their own trash. This fundamental lack produces a twisted form of leadership that causes employees to compete for their own survival in the eyes of the leader, rather than add to the synergy of the company.[2]

Several historians believe that the failure of Richard Nixon's presidency is directly attributable to his not having a coach or mentor to point out his own spin. As Nixon made mistake after mistake, no one was able to show him that he was in a spin until he had lost the White House. Even though each situation seemed different, Nixon's responses to each situation showed a clear pattern that was destined to fail.

It's the job of the coach to get the person she is coaching to "see" the spin—in all of its ugliness. Jay was fortunate enough to realize that his career with that company was over before anyone showed him the door. He quit on his own, taking a similar position in a for-profit manufacturing company.

His good fortune continued when he was assigned to a director who believed in coaching. She worked with Jay once a week, as she did with all her direct reports, to coach them to higher performance. Within a week of Jay's hiring, she began to hear stories about crass jokes. She decided to probe into it. Here's some of what Sandra, the director, and Jay spoke about (notice the "going deep" listening practice in action):

Sandra: What causes you to tell these jokes?

Jay: I just want to be one of the guys.

Sandra: What's so important about being one of the guys?

Jay: I can't manage people who think I'm stuffy.

Sandra: What would make people think you're stuffy?

Jay: I've always been stuffy. My dad was a minister. I was the kid no one would play with. They all thought I wasn't into joking around. You know . . .

Sandra: So when you feel stuffy, you tell a crass joke?

Jay: Well, not always.

Sandra: Most of the time?

Jay: I suppose. I find people connect better with me.

Sandra: Jay, you're hooked on your crass jokes. Do you realize that?

Jay: No, I'm not.

Sandra got to the point where she had established a safe environment and, by "going deep," identified the mental pain that drove Jay's spin. Now what?

Trash Bag to the Rescue

We believe that psychologists do the world a lot of good, but that many psychologists encourage people to keep reliving the pain rather than dumping it into the trash. Coaches can use a very simple, easy-to-use tool.

Think of a trash bag in all its simplicity and brilliance. It doesn't take long for trash to soak through a paper bag or topple out of a trash can that isn't lined with a trash bag. Without these plastic inventions our houses would reek of garbage. There's even more to the trash bag's brilliant simplicity—it can be tied up and everything inside is isolated from the world. All the trash is neatly stored in one place where it cannot leak, seep, or reek.

We encourage managers who are coaching employees to imagine themselves armed with a box of trash bags. The employee is allowed, even encouraged, to vent his ugliest, darkest gripes without being judged for them—or fired for them—and the coach merely collects this trash without letting any of it splatter on him. This is the venting stage of the trash bag tool.

Sandra worked with Jay to help him "see" several important insights. First, he "saw" that his use of crass jokes sprang from his uncomfortable feelings around people. Second, he "saw" that the spin was costing him—and costing him dearly. Third, he "saw" that the spin also benefited him—it reduced his anxiety around people. Fourth, he "saw" how widespread his feelings of separation had become throughout his professional life.

Once the person dumps all the garbage out, the coach asks him to pick up his trash—all of it—and put it inside the trash bag. The coach ties it up. It's trash. The person being coached is informed that he is not allowed dumping privileges any time he feels like it. It's garbage. It's yucky. And it gets all over other people unless it is handled responsibly.

Here's how Sandra worked with Jay:

Sandra: Jay, we're now sitting in a room piled high with trash.
Jay: Yeah, I know.
Sandra: I have a trash bag for it. Are you willing and able to put all this into the trash bag?
Jay: (laughs) I hope it's a big bag!
Sandra: It's big enough for this mess. Are you willing and able?
Jay: I can try.
Sandra: Not good enough, Jay. It's yes or no.
Jay: Okay. I'll do it.
Sandra: This means you're agreeing to separate yourself from this part of your childhood. Are you willing and able?
Jay: It's obviously hurting my career, so yes.

The trash bag tool consists of three steps: venting, and then two declarations made by the employee. The first declaration, which Jay just made, is that the trash is in the bag. He's now ready for the second declaration:

Sandra: Jay, are you willing and able to tie up the trash bag?

Jay: What does that mean, exactly?

Sandra: That you will tie up everything we've talked about and move ahead without it. You can bring an item out of the trash bag only under two conditions: that you tell people you're doing it, and that you put it back when you're done.

Jay: Yes, I'll do that.

Getting him to dump his trash is liberating to the entire working environment. Trash is bad on morale. And when people stop carrying it around, the environment looks better and, frankly, smells better.

Problems like Jay's are like melanoma—the most dangerous kind of skin cancer. Unlike the kind that is easily removed, a tiny melanoma tumor on the surface of the skin can send out fingers that reach down to the bone. The "fingers" send new melanoma cells throughout the body on a suicide mission—to plant themselves in new places and grow. Melanoma often spreads to the brain, where it causes dementia and death.

People sometimes don't like this metaphor. They think it's unnecessarily ugly. But think about the mental pain that sends people into spins. The pain can make people miserable, as it was doing to Jay. It can cost people their entire careers—as happened to Richard Nixon. It can make life crazy for people around them, both at work and at home.

The point of the metaphor is that one session with the trash bag is usually not enough. Like melanoma, one use of the scalpel may not get all of the disease. If the person keeps spinning, one of two things is certain. First, you didn't get all of the trash and you should hunt for the rest. Or second, the person didn't really tie up the trash bag.

How do you know when you've gotten all the trash and it's all neatly tied up? Simple. The person will stop spinning.

Let us now return to our story about George, the senior vice president of media marketing, and his manager, Carlos—known to his staff as "Dr. No." George learned to use the trash bag and cleaned up his own trash. He then began to work with Carlos. The first thing George said when he called Carlos into his first coaching session was not what Carlos expected to hear. "I've really let you and everyone in the department down. I haven't supported you as I should have and I'd like to get past that. But, I expect you to do the same with every individual in this office."

Carlos vented about everyone in the department. How they were lazy, dysfunctional, ineffective, or just plain weird. George encouraged Carlos to get it all out.

After Carlos was finished, George responded. "So who hired all these people?"

Carlos was silent for a long moment.

"I don't understand how this applies." From the look of recognition on his face, his boss did get through. He was now beginning to realize that something had gone terribly wrong. These were not the people he had hired. The people he hired were creative, talented, and distinct. He couldn't see what it was that had changed. But yet, if he had asked anyone on his staff, they could have told him what that was. He couldn't quite mouth the word, but a *duh* was starting to form in the back of his throat.

For all the trouble Carlos was having, he was still the bright, motivated, MBA-trained person George had hired. Carlos "saw" a glimpse of his own spin—he had labeled every single person in the office as inept. He had done it over, and over, and over. "Why am I spinning?" he wondered.

Again, it takes "going deep" to find the engine that is driving the spin. George worked with Carlos in short doses daily over the next two weeks to get him to "see" that Carlos was reliving his early days as an employee. Even though he had been a hip and popular DJ working his way though college, after he graduated he dealt directly with people in a business environment. Unfortunately, Carlos had been unpopular at work, labeled by his peers as "nerdy and geekish," someone who carried an HP calculator around in his shirt pocket. He had also been overweight and his posture made his appearance worse.

In college Carlos had gotten around his self-image problem by collecting dirt on every person around him. As a communications major, Carlos used his verbal abilities to reduce this dirt, and therefore the people around him, to one word—"stupid," "lazy," or "odd." In the college environment as a DJ, this tactic not only worked, it was popular. A college DJ is expected to make waves and deliver radical statements that rebel against the established system. However, the college environment is not the work environment and what works in one may not work in another. This was a big *duh* waiting to happen if Carlos could see it.

So, Carlos successfully retaliated against the nerd/geek label that his peers had hung on him by labeling them as "odd," "stupid," or "lazy" in the eyes of his bosses. This tactic resulted in his promotion at their expense. It looked to Carlos like his "reduce to dirt" tactic worked, so Carlos used it again and again—until it became a spin. Thanks to the effective coaching from George, Carlos "saw" that this way of getting ahead was a false and hollow victory. *Duh.*

So the trash that needed to go into the trash bag was Carlos's own laundry list of insecurities, all rooted in Carlos's doubts about his ability to directly compete with people. He felt odd around them, and used his verbal abilities to deflect his fear and to negatively label people in everyone's eyes—including in his own.

George encouraged Carlos to put all his trash into the bag and to tie it up by making declarations.

Then, again with George's support, Carlos started to straighten things out with his staff, first with a general staff meeting and then, through a series of one-on-one meetings with each person who reported to him. These meetings were both eye-opening and difficult for everyone involved and took considerable courage and commitment on each person's part. It takes a high degree of coaching skill to facilitate meetings when "old feelings" are running high. However, the fact that there are high feelings indicates that people actually care about the job and will be willing to move on if someone skillful will coach them to tie up their trash in a trash bag. The fundamental key is that the established tone of the meetings was one of absolute safety for all. Everyone could speak candidly.

Larry said: "Frankly, Carlos, I'm bored. You promised that I would have the chance to work with you on a lot of exciting projects, but I'm stuck doing the same thing day after day, week after week." Carlos "saw" the effect of his spin and it made him deeply sad.

Josh said: "Every time I try something, I take flack for it. On the other hand, if I don't do anything at all, no one complains." Again, Carlos caught a glimpse of his own trash rubbed into the clothing and skin, contaminating the environment of one of the people he hired.

Kevin said: "That's how we work. We talk about the problems on the staff and get inspired to write plans to fix things. Except we never show those plans to anyone." Brett agreed: "Yeah, you piss all over everything." Maria said she was distracted by all the gossip and she didn't want to close her door the way Mike does all day. She'd go crazy without any feedback. Her problem was that Carlos's feedback was consistently negative, so she started consulting Kevin and Brett.

Mike complained that he was the only one who ever got any work done around here. So, why is he being questioned? "Yeah, but you waste a lot of time," was Carlos's reply. "You do things without consulting with anyone. Two seconds of your time and I can say yes or no and save you a day's worth of work."

"I got tired of waiting for you to get around to talking to me," was Mike's retort.

Richard admitted that he felt insecure because creativity was so valued around the office. Everyone seemed to get along well with each other and he felt out of the loop. So he wanted to stand out as interesting and creative.

In their minds, Carlos had moved from being an encouraging, motivating manager to a tyrant who never listened to them and never talked to them except to complain. They all expressed resentment at the labels they felt had unjustly been hung on them. The peculiar thing was that even though Carlos had never said the label word directly to any of his staff, in the environment of gossip and distrust that he unwittingly fostered, they all knew exactly what he was really thinking. Carlos finally saw that as his trash piled higher and higher, he had less and less ability to manage.

It took over a week, but Carlos vividly "saw" the damaging effect of his personal spin and the resulting dumping of his trash on the staff. It was hard to take it all in, but with George's help, he did. To his credit, Carlos sat down personally with each person on his staff to stop the spin, clean up the trash he had dumped on them and put it into the trash bag.

With his own trash out of the way, Carlos was able—for the first time in years—to work with people without his labels for them getting in the way. He began to "see" Richard's creative abilities, and how they could be put to work for the department. He "saw" Mike's impressive analytical skills.

Carlos had a new "trash-free" perspective from which to view all his employees and learned an invaluable tool to "stop the spin"—his own and that of others. True, it didn't solve the overarching immediate problem of how to position the staff, but within his department, it was a new start for everyone—especially for Carlos.

It might be starting now in your company. A few jokes, a few cartoons, a little idle gossip. To deal with it effectively coaches must learn how to stop the spin and use the trash bag to clean up the garbage that pollutes the workplace.

chapter five

Beyond Balance:

Work/Life Impact

Coauthor Dave Logan was consulting to a defense contractor several years ago where Alex, one of the senior managers, experienced a life crisis: after more than 20 years of what seemed like a stable marriage, his wife left him and took the kids with her. Predictably, within about ten seconds, everyone in the 1,000-person operation seemed to know all about Alex and his marital problem. We've always wondered exactly how people learn about such events so quickly.

In a meeting of the senior managers (a meeting Alex usually attended), the director of the division mentioned that Alex wouldn't be joining the group that day, and said he knew we'd probably heard the news. "It's so sad," he said in eulogy-like tone that we figured he'd practiced before the meeting. Like a highly rehearsed Broadway show, everyone exhibited proper behavior on cue: they all looked down at the mahogany and shook their heads ever so slightly. "Well, let's get back to work," the director intoned after a pregnant moment, obviously glad to be moving on.

As the weeks went by, Alex attended the meeting a few times. When he did, his comments were shallow and poorly prepared, almost as if he were speaking to be heard, rather than to say anything. He attended the meeting less and less frequently. Finally, he was laid off during a round of downsizing. Life moved on.

During this same period of time, Dave was consulting for a high-tech company up in Silicon Valley. One of the key employees in the company, Carl, had behavior that paralleled Alex's—he stopped coming to work as often, would only rarely say anything useful, and really seemed to be struggling. He, too, left the company in a wave of downsizing.

But here the similarities end. Alex's life was out of whack, and he just couldn't muster the energy to become a "change agent" in a defense contractor that was retooling for the private sector. Carl's motivation was quite different, we learned later. He was fed up with his job that he felt had become routine. He pursued employment with another company, and received an offer that he accepted the same day. The competitor didn't give a higher salary, but focused on the one thing that mattered to Carl—the type of work he was doing.

What do these stories have in common? The management of both of these employees showed gross incompetence, in our opinion. Alex's boss initially showed kindness but ultimately, told him to straighten out his problem or move on. Carl's boss simply wrote him off when his performance slipped. In both cases, neither boss went to his employee and acted as a coach—identifying what their lives needed and filling in the gaps.

A year ago, Dave got back in contact with Alex's boss and asked him why he never had a "life chat" with his trusted employee. "I couldn't," he said. "The rules say you can't have those discussions. All I could do was refer him to corporate counseling, which I did. I don't even know if he ever went. You know, concern about liability."

Thankfully, most personnel policies now allow for—and even encourage—coaching discussions. The main ambition we hear from employees and managers across the country is that they want their lives to matter—they want to impact the world in some way. People in Generation X (born between about 1965 and 1980) often don't separate their work lives from their private lives—they want their lives as a whole to matter. And they want to work in places where bosses and rules support them, not hold them back for fear of baseless lawsuits.

It's this desire that we believe is at the core of the coaching revolution rippling across corporate America. Alex needed help getting his life back together—his whole life, not just the hours he gave to the company. Carl was playing too small a role at work, he believed, so he (rightfully) made changes to improve his circumstances.

In both cases, these employees found their ability to impact the world—including their families—was hampered. A world-class boss—a manager with coaching skills—will help them impact the world in the way they intend.

Beyond Balance

At the time of this writing, "work/life balance" is big in the news. Companies that help their employees "balance" home and life are profiled as trendsetters.

Let's think about this balance concept for a moment. According to systems theory, every system—from the human body to plants to the human intellect—seeks "homeostasis," which some people think means the same thing as "balance."

It doesn't. If a system remains in balance all the time, it will almost certainly die. A human baby isn't in balance; it's growing and changing at a breathtaking pace. It's seeking "homeostasis," literally, the "same state" as the adult it is trying to become. To get to this state, it will violate balance—as any parent knows.

Move a plant away from the sun and it spends massive resources to turn itself. Again, it throws balance out when the situation changes.

Think of any person you really admire, and chances are, they violated the balance rule for a good part of their lives—probably the part that made them worth admiring. Attending graduate school, raising a child, starting a business, passing the CPA test—or doing several of these things at once. All of these are ambitions that require us to go beyond the rules of balance. If you're reading this book, chances are you violated balance at some point in your life. There's even a good chance you're doing it now.

Why? Because you want your life to matter, to count for something. You were willing to stretch, miss sleep, learn things that lazier people wouldn't bother to learn.

It's our argument that *everyone* wants a life that counts, but that *everyone* measures life a little differently. For some of us, spending every possible moment with our families is what counts. For others, it's leading a business back to profitability so employees can keep their jobs. Some of us want to become physicians or attorneys or parents or entrepreneurs.

So, in a nutshell, we think that "work/life balance" is an idea whose time has passed. It assumes that life is like a pie—only so big, so nobody better take a big slice. Sure, working parents need support. And people going to school need flexibility. But if life is a pie, its size is determined by the ambitions and the actions of the person living it. Rather than making a piece smaller so another piece can grow, why not just bake a bigger pie?

Another Ineffective Idea

In past decades, organizations seemed to hire "partial people"—the professional part. The personal part was unimportant, or at least off limits for discussion. Any one of us with half a brain knows that we're not effective when we have child care problems, or relationships in trouble. Yet most managers used to be taught that the only "part" of the person that matters is the "part" that's hired.

This notion is a fossil from the *Father Knows Best* era. Robert Young went to work—we were never quite sure where—and then he came home in his suit, smiling, kissed his wife and hugged his kids and became Dad. Dad and Employee are like twins that were separated at birth—two half-persons who never meet.

Today, our careers are much more complicated, not that they were ever as simple as early TV portrayed. In most big companies today, HR professionals have paved the way in undoing old policies and allowing for coaching discussions. Most corporate-wide coaching efforts have been at least partially sponsored by HR—and their companies are reaping the benefits.

A Better Way

Washington D.C.'s Marriott International actually has a director of work/life initiatives. Her name is Donna Klein. She discovered that workers were driven from their jobs usually because of personal problems. For these low-wage workers who changed sheets and scrubbed toilets, and barely eked out a living below the poverty line, such crises as domestic violence, problems with immigration, and homelessness impacted their ability to hang onto their jobs. The turnover rate was a staggering 100 percent or more. Supervisors spent 50 percent of their time helping employees straighten out their personal lives. The sheer economy of the situation demanded action.

Klein established a 24-hour hotline, which provided assistance and referrals from trained social workers. Five years after the program was implemented, the employee turnover rate was reduced to 35 percent, saving the company two million dollars in hiring and training costs. In 600 cases, the hotline was key in keeping the employee from quitting. The company also documented higher morale, increased productivity and improved relations with coworkers and managers.[1]

Ironically, the advocates of the "partial people" idea would argue that lower-wage employees like housekeepers are the ones who suffer from prying managers, and that preserving privacy will protect them.

Undoing the Unintended Consequences

Management theorist Karl Weick writes about the vicious circle in a parable of a tractor and a farmer.[2] The farmer tries to till the ground with a tractor that is so heavy it packs the soil down for the next year. So the farmer buys a bigger tractor, which presses on the dirt even more. And so on. It's the law of unintended consequences—the tractor that was bought to solve a problem makes the problem worse. In general, a "fix" often causes a bigger "break" in the long run.

So far in this chapter, we've examined two "fixes" that have actually broken the system of employment. The first is the view that people's work life and personal life should be balanced, which, like Weick's tractor, made it tougher for people to impact the world—which was their real goal. The other "fix" was preventing managers from even talking with employees about personal issues, which actually damaged a lot of personal lives.

So let's put Humpty Dumpty back together again—this time, with the dumb designs left out. Employees are people, and people want their lives to make an impact. This impact includes work, but isn't limited to work. Some are primarily interested in their families. Others want their career to get most of the attention. Manager-coaches, we believe, should empower employees to succeed. And we argue that "success" should be defined by the employee.

Before moving on, it's important to point out that people do have private lives, and many aren't comfortable with their managers probing in too far. From our observations, common sense is a much better guide for people than policy edicts. Some employees will actually interpret a hands-off approach as noninterest. Others will want coaching, but only on work-related issues.

The key is to create an atmosphere that allows for "life coaching," but doesn't insist on it. We believe that most people are adult enough to work out the details for themselves.

Warning Signs

When people feel they are on the "wrong track"—that is a track that doesn't matter to them and one that spins their lives out of control—certain warning signs emerge. The employee may make a lot of personal phone calls, arrive to meetings and to work late, binge on vending machine food, drink 12 cups of coffee or cans of Diet Coke each day, take too many breaks, look like he or she just rolled out of bed, seem tired, and may often get extremely sensitive. The employee may be frustrated about not being as productive as he or she would like to be. Other warning signs are more subtle—a neat person starts to "pile" work instead of dealing with it when it comes in. They become irritable over trivial things.

These are classic signs of employee burnout. Burnout can happen all at once—and suddenly—or it can smolder slowly for years. Either way, the manager-coach should take these warning signs seriously.

A lot of people will misunderstand these signs. Some will think that the employee doesn't care. Others will think that the problem *must be* work, or that the problem *must be* home. Some will think that they need rest, or that they're just tired. (In actual fact, sleeping too much and irritability are both signs of burnout, and often go together.)

Burnout is tricky, even for experienced manager-coaches. If just one area of life is out of whack, it can drag down every other area. In most cases, the person doesn't know what area is really to blame, because everything seems wrong.

Worker Wanderlust

At the opposite extreme from burnout is wanderlust—unhappy employees leave. From an outsider's perspective, this change sometimes seems odd. For some Microsoft employees who joined the company for the excitement of working for the revolutionary upstart, the thrill is now gone as a federal judge declared this massive corporation a monopoly and ordered its breakup.

One such employee, Michael Ahern, was a top marketer for Microsoft for nine years, having worked on the Windows 95 launch and shaped the company's e-commerce software. He gave up a one million dollar stock option and the chance to be a VP to enter an uncertain future by joining Internet start-up GiftSpot.com.[3] He's risking everything to find adventure at work.

Fortysomething Reed Kingston gave up his comfortable office, secretary, and prestigious client base as an Ernst & Young partner for an office behind a machine shop, no assistant, and no salary for a voice recognition startup. Simply stated, they gave it all up for the chance to impact the world—and satisfy their values—more directly.[4]

If you don't think burnout is a problem for your employees, wanderlust might be. The cure for both is the same—identify what's important to the person, then help them achieve that. When life satisfaction increases, burnout and wanderlust both diminish—and often vanish.

But We All Need to Eat

Many workers are willing to give up a lot for a job and a life that have impact. Others feel they have such jobs, but are torn between them and other areas of their lives that may be just as important.

In a university commencement address several years ago, Brian Dyson, CEO of Coca Cola Enterprises, prioritized family, friends, health, and spirituality above work:

"Imagine life as a game in which you are juggling some five balls in the air. You name them—work, family, health, friends and spirit—and you're keeping all of these in the air. You will understand that work is a rubber ball. If you drop it, it will bounce back. But the other four balls—family, health, friends and spirit—are made of glass. If you drop one of these, they will be irrevocably scuffed, marked, nicked, damaged, or even shattered. They will never be the same."

When Heather D. Blease asked her children whether they wanted her to stay home rather than work in lieu of private school, flashy house, and European vacations, their response was, "Work, Mommy."[5]

But Blease also took care of her family, enough so that her children did not feel deprived of her time. When her company's revenue grew one hundredfold in less than five years, she outsourced many tasks that would otherwise take her away from her children. A housekeeper comes in three days per week. A personal assistant handles the dry cleaning, arranges the dental appointments and schedules the children's activities in addition to administrative duties. This allows Blease to give the better part of her time to her children.

Advice like Dyson's and stories like Blease's inspire a lot of people. Dyson talked about impact and Blease balanced her life like an acrobat.[6] Our aim in this chapter is to help you and your employees to foster both impact and balance in a predictable, planned, and reliable way. The benefits are numerous, and many of them are obvious: greater satisfaction, increased loyalty (a word that's temporarily out of vogue), heightened productivity, and greater morale. We now turn to a tool manager-coaches can use to bring about impact, balance, and these benefits.

The LifeLine Tool

When James Lloyd's dream came true to own his own software development company, Versatile Systems Inc., after years of barely scraping by to support a wife and children, his family benefited from the financial security, but never saw him. His wife had to intervene to set some rules—such as, having him home for family dinners and insisting that he only work half days on the weekends. He had a hard time living up to those rules. His children often teased him about his not knowing who they were. His wife often complained about feeling like a single parent. What Jim didn't realize was that he didn't need to work that many hours.

The office looked much like Jim's home life. He sat on invoices for weeks. He reasoned that he didn't have time to process them and, of course, he was right. What Jim didn't see was that his employees had plenty of time. Jim fell into the classic "founder's syndrome" trap of doing everything himself. He didn't feel that he could trust anyone else to meet his expectations and competence level. Again, in many cases he was right. The question is, was he being right about the right things? After all, he was the one who hired them. When his brother and business partner, Phil, finally opened Jim's eyes to the fact that in terms of hiring, he was a poor judge of character, Jim slowly began to allow others in the company to take care of the hiring.

As the coaching from his brother progressed, Jim found that he was in an ongoing battle with himself. However, once he started to look at his situation objectively, he began to consider that it wasn't necessary for him to do everything. Jim began to find more time to do what mattered most to him and what made him a successful entrepreneur in the first place—software development and sales of value-added products. He found that he could even do this from his home.

Today Jim works four days each week and he knows all seven of his children by name.[7]

Jim was extremely fortunate to have people in his life that helped him "see" where he was neglecting the things and the people that mattered to him. But, as in the earlier cases involving Alex and Carl, not everyone has the advantage of people who care enough and are insightful enough to intervene.

We've developed a tool that helps people "see" their lives measured against their priorities—so that you and your employees don't leave anything to chance. We recommend that people use this tool long before their lives reach a breaking point. But even when things are going wrong—spiraling out of control like some of the stories we've seen in this chapter—it can help people course-correct in the midst of a crisis. We call this the LifeLine tool.

Chart 1.0: The Lifeline Tool

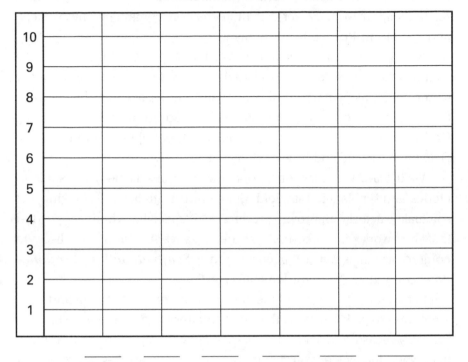

Copyright ©2001 JLS Consulting, Inc.

The LifeLine Tool helps people to "see" how they're doing measured against the kind of impact they want their lives to make.

We recommend that you, as the manager-coach, use the LifeLine tool before you help employees use it. Otherwise, your advice and coaching might drown in the "physician, heal thyself" phenomenon. Like Alex and Carl, other people can tell when someone's life is working well and when it's broken. Manager-coaches have to "get their own house in order," as the cliché goes, before they can help others.

Start by drawing out something resembling Chart 1.0, including the blank lines at the bottom. Next, pick the most important areas of your life. This list can include, but isn't limited to, family, finances, friends, relationships at work, career, health, recreation, community involvement, and spirituality. Pick up to six areas.

Some people are squeamish about picking "spirituality," so let's spend a moment with that. *BusinessWeek* devoted a recent cover story to the topic, as 51 percent of Americans feel modern life leaves them too busy for God, prayer, and spirituality.[8] So businesses are bringing God to them. Bible and Talmud studies are popping up in places like Deloitte & Touche and New York law firms.

We'll leave the question about how this affects people's souls to clerics and scholars in that field. But empirical studies are showing that spirituality actually improves productivity, especially when people feel that they work for employers that are "less fearful, [and] less likely to compromise their values," according to *A Spiritual Audit of Corporate America* by USC Professor Ian Mitroff.[9]

Let's return to the LifeLine tool. It's important for you and your employees to pick the areas that really matter to you, otherwise the tool will only measure trivial issues. If spirituality is important to you, put it in. If your finances or your family or your friends are key areas of your life, put those in. Write the names of these areas on the blank lines below the chart.

Next, notice the numbers along the vertical axis. This is a measure of your satisfaction, ranging from 10 (very satisfied) to 1 (not satisfied at all). Next, stick a dot next to your satisfaction in each area. It's important to rate yourself honestly. In our time of working with managers, we've seen problems perpetuate because the client couldn't admit that a need wasn't being met. Every problem eventually comes to the surface. The only question is whether it will on your timetable, when the problem is small, or if you'll ignore it until it explodes.

Next, connect the dots, so that your LifeLine will look like a stock chart. Virtually no two LifeLines are the same, but yours should look something like Charts 1.1–1.4.

Finally, sit back and answer the question: "What do I 'see' in my LifeLine?" Go through the good, the bad, and the ugly. We'll get to what to do about any problems, but the first step is to "see" your life for what it is.

The first insight you should have is that the areas listed at the bottom of the LifeLine define what work/life impact means for you. Many people struggle for a lifetime trying to identify what areas they should focus on, and what things are secondary. "Seeing" what's important to you is a valuable exercise.

Next, look at the line—the high areas and the low areas. Note whether everything is at the same level, or if it jumps around like a printout of an EKG. Keep in mind that the lowest point on the LifeLine brings everything else down like an anchor. That's the bad news. The good news is that boosting an area on your LifeLine will start a wave of momentum that will pull everything else up.

Let's look at a few real examples of people's LifeLines. Think of this as a short course in medical school. By learning to "read" a LifeLine chart, you'll dramatically improve your coaching skills.

Chart 1.1 shows an employee who is fairly happy, though he admits there is room for improvement. He is a "solid employee." He shows up for work a few minutes early and in a good mood. He is resourceful and good at dealing with problems and staying calm in stressful situations. He probably keeps healthy snacks in his desk so that his energy level stays up. He also brings lunch from home to watch his expenses.

He has his limits, however, and may seem somewhat uncooperative if asked to stay late. He rarely works overtime—except in a pinch. He values his personal time for family and recreation and he makes that abrasively clear when that time is threatened.

Chart 1.1: The Solid Employee

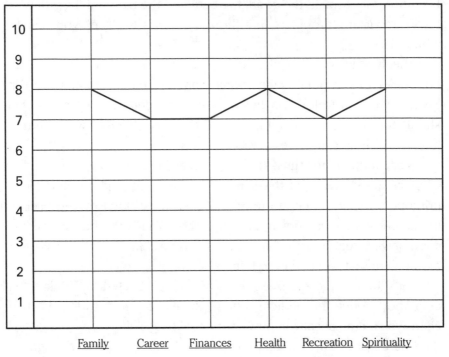

Family   Career   Finances   Health   Recreation   Spirituality

This LifeLine illustrates an employee who has balance in his life and work and is achieving fairly high levels of life impact. Family, friends, health, and spirituality all get about the same amount of attention as work.

Chart 1.2 shows a person with a great deal of dedication at work. She is obviously focused on her career, and her income shows it. She arrives to work early and stays late day after day. She hasn't taken a vacation in years. She's received several bonuses for the extra time she's put in. However, she has a lot of visible problems that everyone sees but her. And her employer doesn't have the heart to say anything.

Chart 1.2: The Workaholic

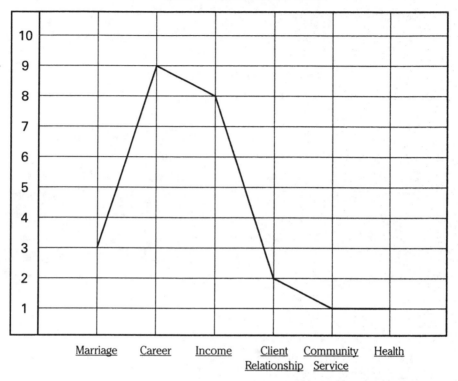

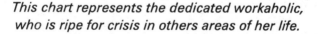

| Marriage | Career | Income | Client Relationship | Community Service | Health |

Copyright ©2001 JLS Consulting, Inc.

This chart represents the dedicated workaholic,
who is ripe for crisis in others areas of her life.

Her appearance is somewhat run down, and that is why she's been excluded from client meetings, a source of frustration for her. She wants her job to impact the community, but more and more she feels the job is controlling her, rather than the other way around. Health is important to her, yet she is too busy to take care of herself, another source of dissatisfaction. She's tired and she looks it. Her husband is practically a stranger to her, but "someday," she reasons, "we will retire together somewhere." She is ripe for a crisis in her marriage, in her health, or both.

Her boss sees it coming and dreads the day when that crisis will yank her out of the job, because she's such a valued employee.

What a quandary for a manager. You know this employee makes your bottom line look good for now, but what will happen when one of the ticking time bombs of her neglected life goes off?

We suggest you don't wait to find out. This employee needs help with issues of family, health, and recreation immediately.

The first step is to get the employee to "see" the problem for herself. Remember the words about change from Ben Cohen—people change when the need for it becomes "self-evident." Encouraging her to chart out her LifeLine is the first step.

When this person looked at her troubled LifeLine, she fired back with "Well, those other things aren't important to me." We pointed out that she had picked them.

"Well, I was wrong," she said, stiffly.

"Well, then, what's important to you?" we asked.

She stared at her LifeLine for a good minute without saying anything.

"These, I guess," she finally admitted, pointing to the areas she had selected.

It sounded like a *duh* to us. She had "seen" her life and was ready to make some adjustments.

The employee represented by Chart 1.3 is just the opposite. This person wants opportunities at work yet bolts out of the office each day right at 5:00. Actually, at 4:45—she sets her clock ahead 15 minutes. Of course, she measures her timeliness to work by her watch, which is set to the correct time.

She spends a lot of time with friends, traveling, going to the theater, and a number of other activities. This person doesn't seem to understand something basic to her life. Why isn't her job as interesting as her hobbies? She also wonders why the boss doesn't give her a promotion or a raise—after all, she needs the money. Her employer would love to

Chart 1.3: The Employee with a Life

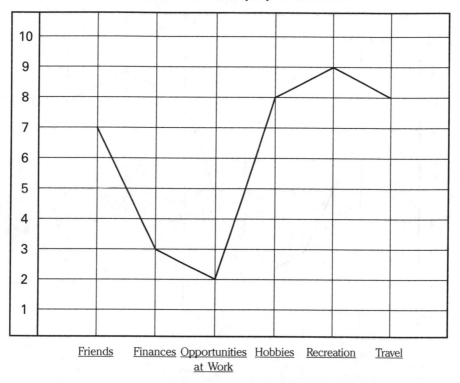

Friends   Finances Opportunities Hobbies Recreation   Travel
at Work

Copyright ©2001 JLS Consulting, Inc.

This is a common scenario for many managers—
an employee who would rather be anywhere but work.

use her more, because she has a professional appearance, she's quick-witted, and is extremely sharp. But, to the boss, she seems to have no interest in or dedication to her job.

She needs to think about what she wants out of work. Perhaps she is in the wrong career. She needs something that competes with her exciting recreational life. Perhaps she needs to combine the two. We didn't have the opportunity to work with her, but our first step would be to do another LifeLine that would focus only on work issues, including

Chart 1.4: The Flatliner

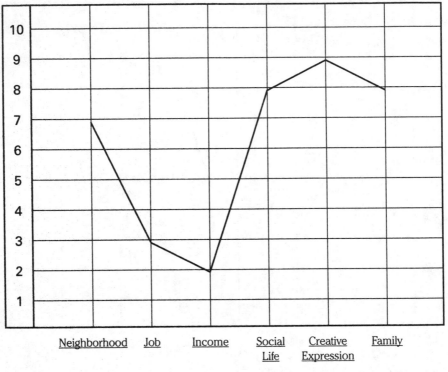

Copyright ©2001 JLS Consulting, Inc.

This employee needs help and encouragement in all areas of his life.

job duties, relationships at work, opportunities for advancement, amount of independence, etc. By "seeing" what is going well and what isn't, she might be able to tweak her job for better enjoyment.

Chart 1.4 is sad. He's concerned with immediate survival—his neighborhood, his job (not a career), and his income—all of which are in the tank. Yet, there is something more to this person's frustration. Perhaps he has a hidden creative talent he would like recognized. Social life is also important to him, yet that too is beyond his grasp.

Perhaps if his manager explored how he could use his creative talents to the company's advantage, he might get a momentum boost that would pull the rest of his life up. Chart 1.4 is typical of employees who are quietly desperate for coaching, but may not know it.

This employee is young—only 20 years old. He barely finished high school and never went to college. His manager, who was really a manager-coach, encouraged him to set small development goals, like taking one class a quarter at the local community college. "Slowly but slowly," his manager told us, his whole life improved. At last report, this employee had transferred to a four-year university and is pursuing a degree in business administration. Good for him! And good for his manager-coach!

Five Levels of Satisfaction

Chapter 3 presented the cultures that appeared in our research and that we've seen over and over in companies around the country. We're now ready to take this idea a step further.

But first, a quick review (notice we've added a column):

Name of Culture/ Effectiveness	Key Theme/ Metaphor of Culture	Employees' Connections with Each Other	Affect and Scope of People's Behavior
Vital	"Life is Great"	Teamwork	Benefits All
Important	"We're Great"	Partnership	Benefits Some
Useful	"I'm Great"	Personal	Benefits Me
Ineffective	"I'm a Victim"	Separate	Hurts Some
Undermining	"Life Sucks"	Alienated	Hurts All

Copyright ©2001 JLS Consulting, Inc.

We've worked with dozens (probably hundreds) of people who picked "health" as one of their LifeLine areas. At least 90 percent put down something from 4 to 8, with the average around a 5 or a 6. When we ask people about health, the folks who put down a 4 or a 5 give reasons why their health is out of their control—"My job makes me work too long and I can never work out or sleep enough," or "I have to pick between my family and my health, and my health loses." People who put down a 6 or a 7 speak very differently—"I jog sometimes, and that keeps my health on track," or "I'm in okay shape." The fortunate few who list an 8 talk about health as if they're part of a club that smart people should join—"My family and I take our health very seriously," or "I'm part of a jogging group at my synagogue."

Notice the connection? When we first noticed it, we were floored—the numbers people list on their LifeLine correlate almost perfectly to the five cultures. People who put down something from 1 to 3 use language like people in the "undermining" cultures—life is just out to get them. "I used to work out, but it didn't do any good. People said it would improve my life. It didn't," was how one person in a recent seminar put it. She rated herself a 2 for health, was at least 100 pounds overweight and took more prescription pills at lunch than we could count. Then she ate more than most three people would eat combined. She talked about her blood pressure, her cholesterol, and problems with depression.

Folks who put down something from 3 to 5 (notice there's a little overlap) use "ineffective" language in describing their situation. This is the group who will say why they can't work out, how their finances are beyond their control, or that their career isn't enjoyable because they don't have enough education. The moment someone tries to tell them otherwise, they respond like a Trekkie at a meeting of the Flat Earth Society—they can "prove," beyond any doubt, that they're stuck and that's all there is to it.

Most managers rate themselves something from 5 to 7 on health, which correlates to "personal." Just as you'd expect, people in this range describe their accomplishments—"I jog," "I'm getting my MBA,"

"I go to church," and so on. Most sentences start with "I" or end in "me." Their language is "personal." They don't encourage others to follow their lead, but rather get an ego boost from their accomplishment.

A few fit people give themselves something from 7 to 9, and they emphasize their allegiance to a group, and often their superiority to people who don't belong to their club. "Our church has a great social connection," or "University of Texas people hang together, you know." There's an "us" and a "them."

When people give themselves a 9 or a 10, they use language like a "vital" culture—there's no "us-them," there's just a strong desire to move ahead. People act more energetic, more enthusiastic, even a little naïve. "I just love what I do, and I enjoy helping others plan their careers," one man recently told us who gave himself a 9 on "career." No "us" or "them," just a passion for helping others.

What amazed us is that we've noticed that people surround themselves with like-minded (and like-speaking) people in just about every area of their life. We just consulted in one nonprofit that had four people who met every morning by the coffee machine to laugh at the *Married with Children* reruns the night before. Three of the four listed "marriage" or "family" as one of their areas and all put down low numbers. They laughed at the sarcasm of the show and often spoke about how it mirrored their lives. They had created a mini-culture in which they all spoke the same language about the same topic. The moment someone tried to interject something positive, eyes rolled and people sighed.

The point of all this is that people tend to surround themselves with others who either revel in their accomplishments or languish in their pain. They literally pick out people who speak the same language about that life area. Aside from this being an interesting insight, it turns out to be the key for enhancing work/life impact.

Think of an area of your life that used to be lower (from 2 through 4) and is now higher (from 7 through 9). Chances are, you not only changed your situation but swapped out a group of complainers for a group of optimists on that subject. We're willing to bet you also changed your theme about that life area—from "I'm a victim" to "We're great," perhaps.

The old adage turns out to be true—"birds of a feather flock together." What we discovered is that if one bird changes its feathers, the other members of the flock will change them back—or kick that bird out. If you're not happy with your feathers, maybe you need to find some different birds to fly with.[10]

Personal Initiatives

For decades, executives have known the importance of initiatives in corporate evolution. Once they recognize a need—such as quality, customer service, or employee satisfaction—they often partner with consultants to plan an initiative that will fix the problem. This is how most "turnarounds" begin. Perhaps the classic of the last century was Lee Iacocca's launching initiative after initiative in Chrysler to restore customer loyalty, streamline production, restructure corporate debt, and reward innovation. Having spent some time at Chrysler (now Daimler-Chrysler), we've seen a lasting effect from the Chairman's Award for Innovation that Iacocca began.

Other initiatives start by identifying an area of strength and then moving to capitalize on it. Sam Walton realized he had a new model for retailing that was better than anything out there, so he launched an expansion initiative that gave birth to your local Wal-Mart.

The reason we bring up these examples is that most executives are brilliant at coming up with corporate initiatives, but most don't apply this brilliance to personal issues. Including their own personal issues, unfortunately.

A personal initiative is just like a corporate initiative, but it's designed to boost the impact of your life in the areas you choose. It consists of an action, or a series of actions, that will propel your satisfaction in at least one area. The goal should be to jump by at least one cultural layer—from "personal" to "important," for example. A change of just one number will keep you locked in the same culture, and members of a culture have a knack for keeping their members from changing.

Our advice is to use this formula in coaching your employees:

1. What do you "see" in your LifeLine?
2. Pick an area. What's something you could do to boost that area of your life by at least three numbers?
3. What exactly would that "look like"?

Coach people until they have a specific plan—an initiative—for how to improve that area. People will be tempted to come up with something costly—either in terms of time or money—that will collapse under its own weight. Spending two hours a day at the gym probably won't happen or it would have already happened. Going from not doing any professional development to a full-time doctoral program is equally unrealistic.

Help people identify "quick fixes," or the "low-hanging fruit." And just so we get all the biz clichés out, the "quick wins," "the slam dunks," and "the easy victories." Walking for 30 minutes at lunch three times a week is more realistic. Cutting out the doughnuts is more likely to happen. Reading *BusinessWeek* every week is easier than taking 128 units toward a B.S. in accounting.

Why Change Doesn't Happen

Management theory is filled with examples, models, and explanations for why change is hard. Whether you've studied these theories or not, you probably know why change doesn't happen—because systems resist change. New York City had a devil of a time cleaning up its streets. IBM almost failed to retool to serve the PC world. Why? Because egos, careers, and power are on the line. Egos, careers, and power don't like change.

The manager-coach who helps employees visualize a change but doesn't help them follow through has actually done damage. The result will likely include cynicism, a "been there, done that, got the T-shirt" mentality. It will make change harder in the future.

Follow-through on personal initiatives is hard because cultures fight change. Think of it as the sound barrier—there's a huge turbulence field between ineffective and personal, and between personal and important. That turbulence is filled with nay-sayers, pessimistic jabs, and caustic comments from people in the culture your employee is trying to leave.

For this reason, we advise managers to work with employees until they have left the old culture, moved to the new culture, and then planted themselves. This means swapping one social network for another, and replacing one vocabulary with another. Once the person is settled, they'll be able to sustain themselves.

The Overtime Trap

Before concluding this chapter, there's one myth we have to discredit, because it's the most-cited reason for not following through on personal initiatives. The myth is that the more time you spend at work, the more work you get done and the more valuable you are to your employer.

Such was not the case with Megan, the sole accountant for an advertising agency. She complained during the lunch hour about how she always had to stay and work until 9:00 every night. Megan openly showed resentment toward Dana, the media buyer who always left work by 5:30 P.M. Dana, however, produced the greatest bottom-line results of anyone at the agency. What was even more amazing about Dana is that she had a life—a husband, two kids, and a resume of more community service than most Scoutmasters.

While she was at work, Dana focused on work and didn't complain. With Megan, the longer she would stay at work the night before, the more tired she would be the next day and the longer it would take her to focus on work. Not only did her work suffer, her relationships and personal life suffered.

Like many people in "ineffective" cultures, Megan's work impact was stunted by her belief that she was a victim. Her overtime actually fed a vicious circle—like Karl Weick's tracker. The longer she worked, the more "proof" she had that she was stuck. The more stuck she was, the more hours she worked. The problem wasn't her hours at all—it was the fact that she was in the overtime trap.

No doubt, to make an impact at work, you and your employees will have to work long hours. Make sure, though, that long hours don't turn into a martyr's symbol, or evidence that someone has been victimized.

This chapter has included some of the most important, and subtle, concepts that you can use to make the leap from a manager to a manager-coach. By helping employees to identify what "life impact" means to them, to "see" their lives against these priorities, and design personal initiatives to increase the impact of their lives, you will truly serve the people around you.

We'll end on a self-serving note: you will also become one of the most sought-out managers in your company. No matter what functions you oversee, you'll find that people in "sexier" areas will want to work for you. We've actually seen people give up salaries and titles to work for a person who believed in life impact. Let's be honest—we all want our lives to count. If you build this fact into your management style, you will truly have become a manager-coach.

part two

Say

When CEO Louis Gerstner took a realistic look at IBM in the midst of the Internet explosion, perhaps without even realizing it, he took the next step in coaching that helped his company realize its full potential.

He called together an Internet task force and together the group "said" that the company would have to reprioritize all its budgets. Within four weeks, the company reallocated $300 million and created the Internet division. Internet sales for IBM were expected to top $12 billion before the end of 1999.[1] IBM transformed itself into a premiere e-business and exceeded those expectations—e-commerce sales reached $14.8 billion in 1999. Not too shabby.

What Gerstner and his task force did was to "say" the potential once they saw it. They saw that they needed to harness the new technology and mold it to what they did best—service. After seeing this, they "voiced" that they would take appropriate action.

Manager-coaches know the power of the spoken word. From Martin Luther King's "I Have a Dream" speech inspiring racial tolerance and national healing to President Kennedy's challenge to travel to the moon, words were always the foundation for realizing untapped potential.

In the next three chapters, you will learn how to empower employees through declarations, how to involve employees in defining corporate values, and how to make the most out of complaints.

chapter six

The Secret to

Leadership

Coauthor John King's e-mail address is *kingofla@earthlink.net*. We're not saying this so you'll send him jokes. Dave, the young task-master, says John reads too many jokes at work as it is.

No, the point of saying this is that he is the King of L.A. People call him "the king," and his "title" has taken on a life of its own. People who don't know the true story behind his title still "recognize" it. They grant that title a certain power, even if, in the end, it's really just the power of our own amusement. The story is worth repeating, however, because it illustrates something useful, and something that's often overlooked in management.

In an earlier career John was a dancer, a choreographer, a producer and director in both stage and television. He had a great time and met all kinds of fascinating people. Most of them taught him a lot.

John visited Iran on a tour with a French rock star for whom he had choreographed a show, and in which he appeared as a principal dancer. This was 1978, when the Shah was still hanging on to power, but, by then, it was clear that the revolution was coming, and coming soon.

They were to perform for the Shah and his extended family; it was Persian New Year and the official celebration of the Shah's son's birthday.

When they reached Iran, they had already toured Japan and other parts of the Middle East, and by the time they got to Tehran they were a tired bunch of performers. People were getting on each other's nerves, and, as in any close company, everyone knew everything about everyone else. Some of what people knew about each other wasn't especially flattering. Some of the performers knew John as a guy who liked to cause a little trouble. We still know him that way today.

They took a bus to the Shah's compound. Security was tight and everyone had to submit to a pat-down search and a thorough search of all bags and belongings. John had recently bought a camera, and the guard asked him to surrender it.

"No problem," John said. "I'd like a receipt."

The receipt, apparently, was a problem. But the camera was new and he wasn't just going to hand it over. He wanted to make sure he'd get it back.

"Give me your camera," said the guard again in as much English as he could muster. Not without a receipt. Soon, his fellow performers were milling about, and he could hear (in his own crude understanding of French) something about "John causing a *scandale*" and something about "*encore.*"

Soon enough, out came a man of about 6'4", 240 pounds, and wearing a Colonel's uniform. This was a rather imposing man. And he was plenty upset that his underling couldn't get him to give up the camera. So he berated the poor guard and then turned to John. "You must give up the camera. These are difficult times; anyone could conceal a bomb inside a camera." Of course, he replied that he would be happy to hand over the camera as soon as he got his receipt.

"This is the home of the Shah of Iran," the Colonel said, "we will not give you a receipt, and to ask is to do great insult to the Shah. Do you wish to insult the Shah of Iran?"

"Listen," John said. "I don't care. I'm the King of L.A., and I want a receipt!"

A few moments later, receipt in hand and free of his camera, he joined his fellow performers inside the palace. Inside, the scene was almost beyond description. Original paintings from the world's great masters—both living and dead—adorned the walls alongside exquisite tapestries. The furniture was so beautiful it seemed like sitting on it would be a crime. And in the banquet hall, the food spread out like nothing John had ever seen before. Fruit, vegetables, mountains of caviar, meats, you name it, everything anyone could want was all there.

The Royal Cousins sat at a long table, including the Shah's son, whose birthday they had come to celebrate. After a few minutes, everything suddenly came to a stop, and all the cousins turned their attention to a grand door. In walked the Shah and his wife. This was the single most elegant couple John had ever seen. She wore a dress of heavy satin, embroidered with pearls and emeralds. He, of course, wore a simple but extraordinary tuxedo. All the cousins lined up—by rank, no less—and greeted their patriarch with the highest ostentation and most obsequious gestures imaginable.

After all these greetings were finished, the Colonel who had issued the receipt for John's camera approached the Shah and whispered something in his ear. The Shah then stepped over to the star of the show and greeted her warmly before stepping back. Then the Colonel approached the Shah again to whisper, and they both turned to face John. He felt his friends and fellow performers back away from him, and he stood there, alone, as the Shah of Iran walked toward him. There he was in this elegant setting, wearing his finest tuxedo, royalty standing erect, a martini in hand, and armed guards all around. It was a James Bond moment.

At the time, he was afraid he was about to die.

The Shah walked toward John with the menacing Colonel by his side. The Shah stuck out his hand.

"I understand you're the King of L.A.," he said as he shook John's hand. "I'm the Shah of Iran. It's nice to meet you."

And that is how John became the King of L.A. by the power of his own declaration, and with the endorsement of an international authority figure.

How Leaders Get to Lead

Lots of people look at the great leaders of the world—whether they're political leaders, top military leaders, great athletes, or high-level corporate leaders—and wonder how they got there. For a great number of people, how leaders become leaders seems to be one of the deep mysteries of the world.

Most leaders become leaders by declaring that they will lead. Most of the leaders in the high tech world simply declared that their products and services were needed—at a time when most people didn't agree. Jobs and Wozniak in the garage building the first Apple, Dell snapping peripheral boards into computer cases to fill an order, a team at Netscape programming a new invention called a "browser."

So what exactly does it mean to make a declaration?

In the early part of the twentieth century, one of the greatest minds of all time, Ludwig Wittgenstein, wrote about "ordinary language philosophy."[1] It gained the attention of J. L. Austin, who had a protégé named John Searle. Searle summarized the work of his mentor and Wittgenstein in a new line of thinking called "speech acts."[2]

One of the "speech acts" Searle wrote about is when people declare something for which no evidence exists. The American Founding Fathers *declared* that they were independent when every piece of evidence said they were not. Lincoln *declared* the slaves were free when his actual authority didn't reach into the American south. In both cases, people made themselves leaders through an "act" of declaration.

Let's return to Wittgenstein for a moment. Not only did he plant the seeds of what his intellectual descendent Searle would call "declarations," but he used the power of declarations in his own career as well. When he was in his early twenties, he studied under the great mathematician Bertrand Russell at Cambridge. He then left his studies to fight in World War I. After being taken prisoner by the Italians, Wittgenstein wrote what would later become one of his most famous books. After the "war to end all wars," he moved from odd job to odd job, including teaching elementary school in lower Austria and serving as a gardener's assistant in a monastery. Now in his thirties, he decided to start again on his doctorate and returned to Cambridge as a research assistant. The rules dictated that he would have to complete his basic research again (since so many years had passed) and then write a dissertation. Instead of following the rules, Wittgenstein declared that he was, in fact, done with his studies. To support his declaration, he pointed to his time with Russell as his research and to his book as his dissertation. The faculty agreed, and he was awarded his doctorate just a few months after starting.[3]

Searle's insights are gaining a lot of attention in corporations today.[4] The act of declaring one's leadership is one of the foundations of good management, it turns out. It's not an exaggeration to say that most of today's business leaders became leaders through an act of declaration.

Steve Jobs re-entered Apple Computer after Macintosh sales had fallen to the point where many analysts were saying the computer company might not survive.[5] Jobs had a reputation of possessing the rare ability to "see" what people wanted—even when people didn't know that they wanted it. His original partnership with Steve Wozniak had produced the first personal computer for the home market. When the original Apple II computers were rolling off the primitive assembly lines, Jobs declared that this new invention would change the world. At first, his declaration seemed to make him the victim of "nerd" and "geek" labels. One executive at IBM—C. Michael Armstrong, now the head of AT&T, said that personal computers wouldn't amount to much.

Yet Jobs continued to behave as if his declaration were still fact—even though most available evidence didn't support him. If public opinion were a courtroom, even Johnnie Cochran couldn't have saved him from a "guilty" verdict.

The Apple II computer became the most successful personal computer of its day. Now with a proven track record, Jobs declared that the future of computers involved "user friendly" interfaces, but the world was skeptical about the first Macintosh. It was slow, only in black and white, and crashed a lot. Still, it was the beginning of the evidence to support Jobs's latest declaration. When Jobs left Apple years later, the Macintosh had overtaken the Apple II as the leader of the industry—with Intel, IBM, and Microsoft scrambling.

We can learn something interesting about declarations by examining what happened next in Jobs's career. He left Apple (some would say he was forced out) to head up NEXT, a computer company that was never successful. Back at Apple, the computer's Newton division—which had been started by Jobs's vision of handheld computers—was struggling. Had Jobs lost his touch?

Looking, back, it's obvious that Jobs was still Jobs—he went on to "save" Apple once again by retaking the helm and introducing the I-Mac.

Yet history records that several of his declarations about the future of technology—declarations that turned into the Newton and NEXT—were wrong.

This is the risk of leadership. It starts with a declaration. If you're successful, people around you will start to agree, and they'll make declarations in support of yours. But this doesn't always happen, and the person making a failed declaration often looks foolish.

To put it bluntly, this is where backbone comes in. People we all admire—Lincoln, Washington, Churchill from politics—Jobs, Gates, Armstrong from corporate leadership—have all made empty declarations that make them look, well, less than stellar. Lincoln said he'd win political race after political race, and lost. Churchill said he'd win several battles that were absolute failures. Gates said the actions of Microsoft were simply leadership; the Justice Department called it monopolistic.

So what's the answer? It comes down to a choice that you have to make for yourself. If you want to develop into a manager-coach, to grasp the reins of leadership in your company, the path to success is through declarations. Yet that path is littered with pitfalls, potential embarrassments, even people laughing at you.

Through Door A is your role as a leader of world-class championship teams—if you learn the art of declarations and the other strategies in this book. Through Door B is mediocrity. We advise managers to think this through very carefully, to talk it over with their families and friends, before committing to a career with risks.

But as something to weigh, we offer a quote that has inspired us every step of the way—from pursuing advanced degrees to running seminars involving tens of thousands, to creating a business partnership that would determine our future and the future of our employees. Here's the quote:

"For better it is to dare mighty things, to win glorious triumph, even though checkered by failure, than to take rank with those poor spirits who neither enjoy much nor suffer much, because they live in the gray twilight that knows not victory nor defeat."[6]

With the hope that you'll pick the career path that will steer you away from Theodore Roosevelt's "gray twilight," let's look at one of the classic leadership examples of all time. Alexander the Great didn't luck into conquering the better part of the known world. He *declared* that he would lead Macedonia to political and military prominence. Of course, Alexander's declaration alone didn't get him all the way through Persia and beyond. Saying that he would do it probably got him laughed at. But had he not said that he would take Macedonia to the ends of the earth, he would certainly never have been known as Alexander "the Great." In fact, he probably wouldn't have been known as Alexander the Anything.

Another classic example of a declaration at work comes from President Kennedy, who said that by the end of the 1960s, America would put a man on the moon, and would bring him back alive. At the time, the statement was almost laughable. Most of the technology we would need didn't even exist. But Kennedy's declaration led the way toward what remains a phenomenal achievement in the exploration of space.

A declaration alone doesn't finish the job. A declaration might set the objective. A startling declaration—like Kennedy's statement about going to the moon—can be inspirational. But what's next?

Alexander the Great didn't march through Persia and deep into India on his own, planting Macedonian flags and singing "this land is my land." He took a whole bunch of people with him, and routed army after army in battle. Somehow, he got all those people to go with him, and he inspired such loyalty and such devotion to his cause that no small number of them died for it. Obviously, somehow, many of these people had to agree with what Alexander said would happen. Many others quite likely thought Alexander was nuts, and that he could never accomplish what he said he would. Some probably went along with him anyway, perhaps simply because his declaration was so audacious that they had to see what would happen.

Two things attract people to a leader: agreement and curiosity. People who are curious, though, eventually will either have to join the team—in other words, *agree*—or move on.

From Declaration to Common Goal

The Major League Baseball season is long. Teams play 162 games between April and the end of September. During Spring Training, many of those teams meet and set the tone, or the context, for their season. Among the better teams, a player might stand up and say, "This team will win the World Series." Among other teams, the declaration might be, "We're going to make the playoffs." The leaders on those teams, when they are effective, end up with a whole team that shares the same goal. In other words, they have plenty of agreement. On those teams, the manager's job, and the jobs of all the other coaches, are easier: everyone shares the same goal already, and everyone agrees that it's worth playing their heart out. What initiates getting those teams to that point of agreement is the audacious declaration made by one bold member of the team.

Managers in business, rather than baseball, often don't realize that their jobs would be easier if they encouraged the people with whom they work to become leaders. Manager-coaches know that they are simply the "leader of leaders," and they make it their business to pro-mote and encourage leadership all around them. Some managers might be threatened by the idea that the people working under them in the corporate hierarchy could become leaders. Wouldn't they simply take the manager's job? A manager who is threatened in this way might even undermine the people he works with, either by preventing them from making declarations, or by blocking any potential agreement with them.

The results of this type of management are generally unfortunate. People whose natural leadership is blocked become frustrated, even cynical. The environment around a manager who blocks the leadership of others, whether he's doing it consciously or not, is poisoned. The best people around him will leave, probably sooner, not later. The manager may think that he's protecting his turf quite effectively, but in fact, he's slowly committing career suicide.

Manager-coaches recognize that many of the best people working with them are natural leaders, and they constantly encourage these leaders' declarations and the agreement they build around them.

Manager-coaches also know that success breeds success, and that the more people accomplish, the more it is possible for everyone to accomplish. Thus, the more a manager's team members lead one another to succeed, the more that success reflects on the manager-coach, and the more successful, influential, and powerful that manager-coach becomes.

A Declaration Isn't the End— or Even the Beginning

Let's back way up. We've seen how a well-timed declaration can change the world—establish what is now the world's oldest democracy, create the first conglomerate, free the slaves.

But making the declaration is actually the second step. The first step is to "see" the world in a different way. George Bernard Shaw phrased it well in *Back to Methuselah*: "You see things; and you say 'why?' But I dream things that never were; and I say 'why not?'"[7] Similar words were used by Robert Kennedy in an address to the Irish Parliament in Dublin, June 1963. After his assassination, Edward Kennedy summarized his brother's unique vision of the world in a moving eulogy.

The manager-coach starts the process of declaration by establishing an atmosphere of openness and trust, then listens like a coach, including "listening for" a person's true values and deep motivations. The manager-coach also listens for differences in what people say is important and their actions. When people "see" their potential, they often blurt out the word *aha* or *wow*. When people "see" that their actions are not in line with their vision, they often let a *duh* fall out of their mouths.

Lincoln realized that a nation with "freedom" as its founding value couldn't empower slavery. *Duh*. Kennedy "saw" that America's push toward innovation *required* that Americans reach the moon first. *Aha*. Reagan knew that the reforms in the Soviet Union would bring pressure on Gorbachev to free East Germany, and that the world must change. *Wow*.

In each case, these insights—what they "saw"—was followed by a declaration—what they "said." For Lincoln, it was signing the Emancipation Proclamation. For Kennedy, it was forcefully uttering the words: "we shall send a man to the moon . . . and return him safely to the Earth" before the end of the decade. For Reagan, it was reframing his declaration as a challenge: "Mr. Gorbachev, tear down this wall!"

As we'll see in the next section, leaders—including manager-coaches—follow up with action—what they "do." Let's look at how a pioneer in the manager-coaching arena did all three.

Harold Geneen, mentioned in Chapter 4, grew ITT from a small business to one of the first major American diversified corporations, or what he called "a unified-management, multiproduct company." How did he do it?

In an article written shortly before his death in 1997,[8] he declared that the company would grow 10-15 percent every year—whether times were good or not. He based this declaration on something that was missing in business up to that time: consistent growth, over the years, no matter what happened in the economy. He realized that a company's executives were paid to grow the company, not to make excuses about why the company couldn't grow. *Duh*.

Much of ITT's growth came through acquisitions, so a big part of Geneen's job was to sit down with the management of an acquired company and get them to "see" his insight and then to agree with his declaration about 10-15 percent growth. He would do this in a formal dinner setting. After the plates were cleared away, he would chat with the new members of ITT about what he expected from them, and how they could live up to his expectations.

As one of the twentieth century's first manager-coaches, Geneen quickly realized that a declaration without follow-through dies the moment it's said. He had to "do" things consistent with what he "said." In the same article, he wrote about the other half of his job: unlocking the fears that bound people in what he called "chains of insecurity." He did this through extended conversations in which he listened for their untapped potential. He would point out their potential and how they could use it to bring his declarations to life. At the end of his life, Geneen looked back and realized that his declarations of 10-15 percent growth of ITT were now penned into the history of business. It started with a declaration and it was supported with follow-up coaching sessions in which he empowered the people around him to become leaders—to make their own declarations that would support his vision, and to follow up with the people around them.

Whose Power Is It, Anyway?

Lots of managers think that their power is something to be hoarded, to protect and defend against attack. But manager-coaches know that the more power they give to the people around them, the more powerful their own coaching becomes. So they use the natural power of declarations as one of their most effective tools.

Manager-coaches encourage their team members to declare a vision that's consistent with everyone's Core Values. It might not be doubling a company's revenue in five years, or landing a man on the moon, or conquering Persia (we discourage managers from engaging in foreign military campaigns), but it should be clear that often the most auda-cious declarations create the most impact. Then, the manager-coach can use the tools presented here, such as listening like a coach, to create and maintain agreement around the original declaration. Much of the time, this can involve getting out of the way.

Alexander the Great couldn't have conquered the better part of the known world without empowering the leaders who answered to him. He had to give them the power to make declarations of their own and to enlist others in the service of these goals. Chances are that the most successful of Alexander's subordinate leaders empowered their junior officers to do the same, and so on down the line. All the way down, then, Alexander's people had ownership in his vision, because it was their own vision by virtue of his and their own declaration.

One of the best places to work, according to several recent surveys, is Levi-Strauss, the company that practically invented jeans. It's a company that violates a lot of the rules people learn in an MBA program. Growth is not always the main objective at Levi-Strauss. The role of an executive is to support the vision of people "beneath" them (on the organization chart).

Levi-Strauss's Robert Haas leads the ethics training in his company. His goal is to take ethics out of the stratosphere (where it sits with phi-losophy and does people very little good) and implement it into the day-to-day decision making at Levi-Strauss. His reasoning is that it's easy for people to feel strongly about ethics—in the abstract sense—but abandon an ethical focus as soon as it's time to do real work. He "saw" that most people decide what's important, then do whatever they feel is right, abandoning their ethics in the process. *Duh.* Haas followed up this insight with a "say" declaration about how Levi-Strauss would do its work: it would do everything honestly, follow through on its promises, use fairness at all times, respect others, show compassion for everyone, and use integrity in all situations.

Levi-Strauss had several contractors who employed underage workers—a direct violation of the ethical declaration of the company. At Haas's direction, Levi-Strauss agreed to pay for books, tuition, and uniforms for the underage workers. Also, the company offered them jobs in the plants once they became of age, but required the contractors to pay the underage children their salaries and benefits while they attended school full time. As a manager-coach, Haas incurred the short-term costs of drilling his declarations into the company's operations, but gained the long-term benefits of a sterling reputation. In 1999, when protesters targeted the Gap for stocking merchandise made by slave labor and underage workers, Levi-Strauss was largely unaffected because Haas coached people to make his declarations a reality.[9]

A shorter, older, and bolder story comes from history, and we'll end this chapter with this example. Charlemagne, the best-remembered Holy Roman Emperor, knew about the power of declaration. At the time he took the throne, it was understood that only the Pope could crown the Emperor, and that without the Pope's decree, no one could be king. Charlemagne, however, took the crown from the Pope's hands, placed it on his own head, and declared himself the Holy Roman Emperor. "Thanks, Pope, for holding on-to my crown."

How many Alexander the Greats are sitting in cubicles right now? How many Charlemagnes? What could be different in your company if you encouraged them to claim their own place in history, starting with a "say" declaration stemming from what you help them "see"? What if you, the manager-coach, led the way to your team members' natural leadership?

While you're considering that question, here's another. Where have you given your own power away by thinking that it comes from some external sources, like those higher up on the corporate ladder? Perhaps your job, as a manager-coach, is to find your own version of Charlemagne's crown, and to claim it. Manager-coaches who do this can tap the authority of that crown to inspire others, and to empower them to declare their own leadership.

Who's holding *your* crown? We suggest you stop reading now and go get it.

chapter seven

Values to the Core

Marc cleaned out his office on a Tuesday afternoon, and walked away from the small software development company he'd joined less than a year before. He left his keys, company identification, and the monarch-sized card with the company's mission statement on his desk.

The bottom of that card once read, "People are our most important asset." Marc left the card with what he considered a "slight correction." Now it said, "People are our most abused asset."

Marc moved on to a new company, but took his ill feelings with him. He's a highly paid software development professional, and he's also a professional cynic. "The only boss you can really trust," Marc says, "is the one you work for when you're self-employed. And I'm not all that sure about him, either."

We've all met Marc in our own offices, in almost every one of our jobs. There are those of us who may have even *been* Marc, at least from time to time. But what makes Marc the software developer become Marc the cynic? And if our offices are full of Marcs, might we be losing productivity? How far is it from there to lost market share, lost profitability, and lost jobs?

We could just get rid of Marc and everyone like him. It's easy enough: round up all the cynics and maligners and fire them. Keep the happy people, and move right along. But of course, in the real world it's not that simple, and, in the words of leadership guru Warren Bennis, "You can't shrink your way to greatness."[1] So now what? If our offices are full of cynics, and if their ranks are swelling, what can we do?

Let's go back to Marc's "corrected" note. It's simple enough to see that Marc believed that the actions of his managers belied the company's mission statement. "People are our most important asset," it said. Yet clearly Marc felt that his bosses not only failed to live up to that lofty statement, but that their actions directly contradicted its spirit.

"After a while," Marc said, "the project managers didn't respect the people actually doing the work. They made ridiculous promises to potential clients, and then when we got the contracts, we, the workers, would either have to meet these insane deadlines, or we, the company, would look like idiots. People were routinely working eighteen- and twenty-hour days trying to keep up with the deadlines, but burning out instead. Gee, what a surprise. And then, of course, people were exhausted and started making mistakes, and we delivered a few projects late, or with problems. After a while, it just seemed like none of us could do anything right. The managers were on our backs night, day, and weekends. We had no life. It was a lot less fun than a poke in the eye with a sharp stick, if you catch my drift."

Pushing Toward Achievement

In Greek mythology, Sisyphus stands out as an unlucky fellow. You'll recall that Sisyphus had the job of pushing a huge rock to the top of a hill. Every time he finished the task, the rock would roll down the hill again, and Sisyphus would return to the bottom to start all over.

Sisyphus accomplished his goal many times, but the achievement didn't last, and it was empty.

People at work often feel like Sisyphus, pushing their own rock up a steep grade, only to watch the boulder roll back down, or to find they've left other rocks unrolled. Think of the times you've wanted to get somewhere, or to attain something, only to find that when you've achieved the goal, you're not satisfied.

We know people who set goals to become corporate vice presidents. They worked like a rabid dog and made manager. They whipped their sales staffs until the department exceeded all the corporate metrics. Some of their direct reports made manager. They made director, then associate vice president. Finally, the magic day came—an e-mail announcement of their promotion to full VP. For about five minutes, life was perfect.

Then the rocks started rolling back down the hill. Only after their promotions did the full cost of their actions stare them in the eyes. While the sales department was busy smashing records, other departments blazed up with worker protests because of disorganized systems.

Once the cost of driving catches up with them, their reputations are tarnished forever. The rising stars have become asteroids burning up in the atmosphere—a temporary glow that people rarely remember.

This effect isn't limited to just careers—it can consume companies. In 1998, coauthor Dave Logan was teaching a second-year elective class in USC's Marshall School of Business. The students he had that semester were widely regarded as among the brightest in the MBA program. He gave them an assignment to analyze companies and recommend a stock as a short-term buy. So when three of them recommended the same stock, it got his attention.

The company was Cendant Corporation—a franchiser created through the merger of two companies—discount-shopping-club operator CUC International and franchising giant HFS Inc. The new Cendant Corporation appeared every day on CNBC's list of "Widely Owned Stocks." So he bought in and felt like a genius. After all, three top MBA students, CNBC's list, and his own good judgment can't be wrong.

Then the bill of his own arrogance came due when the company disclosed that CUC had exaggerated—no, fabricated—earnings.[2] Institutional buyers turned into institutional sellers. How bad can it be, he thought? Very bad, came the answer. He sat on the stock as it rode down from the 30s to about 6.

So what's the point? Cendant couldn't keep up the front forever. Eventually, our short-term victories won at the expense of long-term value turned into visions of hell. Like Sisyphus's rock, it tumbles back down the hill and we're back to where we started. Or worse.

The problem isn't with the achievement itself. Achievement is a great thing. It's fundamental to our economy and our quality of life. The problem is with the way we achieve what we do.

It's the same problem Marc noticed in the management of his company. It's the problem of people who don't align what they do with their Core Values.

Watch for Falling Rocks

As high-achieving people, and as managers, we tend to say, "I want *that*," whatever that is: a new client, a promotion, a sales record, and so forth. Then we look for the strategy that will reach that goal in the least possible time, with the greatest efficiency. We may honor ethical or moral guidelines (at least we hope that you do), or perhaps we will subtly betray these if we feel that the benefit of reaching the goal exceeds the potential damage in getting caught "cheating."

We start to push the rock. Perhaps the client calls with changes, and the hill gets a little steeper. We push harder. If more obstacles arise, we push harder, forcing our rock over them. We finish the project, deliver the product, and then move on to the next one. In other words, we go back down and start pushing another rock.

It doesn't take long for a cycle like this to become unfulfilling, boring, and frustrating. Even if the cycle is filled with achievement, over time all we'll be able to see is the rock rolling down to the bottom of the hill. Or perhaps, we'll simply be worn out in our never-ending effort to keep that rock moving up the hill, just like in Marc's case at the software company.

To Cendant's credit, it has moved ahead despite the setback and is back on most analysts' list of top recommendations. Unlike most companies and many, many people, Cendant learned from its mistakes. At the time of this writing, the company is integrating "integrity" as a Core Value into its system of management, from its board of directors on down.

This brings us to coaching. As a manager-coach, you've already learned to "listen" people into "seeing" insights. You know all about those four magic words—*duh, aha, wow,* and *shazam.* You know how to encourage people to make declarations.

With this as a background, we can now turn to one of the most powerful tools a coach has—to help people become who they really are. To help people discover their own Core Values and work with them to create a way to live out those Core Values in their work environment. Some people can't even entertain this topic until the rocks drop on them. It is a strange thing, but sometimes, very smart people don't have insights or realizations regarding their Core Values until a ton of boulders has dropped on their heads. This is one reason why it is a good thing to have a coach. Often the coach can see the rocks tumbling down the hill and can advise you on how to personally avoid being squashed. But, I digress.

You might be reading this book at a time when the rocks have already fallen. If so, it's not too late. Cendant has pulled itself from scandal back to a position of prominence on Wall Street. Winston Churchill recovered from an embarrassing military defeat and being the man everyone loved to make fun of, to become the greatest and most inspiring Allied leader during the darkest days of World War II.

Ironically, if you're reading this book and times for you are good, and times for the people around you are also good, then you may have a tough road ahead trying to implement what we're about to suggest. Isn't it the truth, that during the good times, we tend to forget the bad times? We tend to think that we've got something handled. The tendency toward this way of thinking is so strong that, in fact, many consultants actually encourage executives to *create* a crisis before taking this next step, if one doesn't already exist.

We disagree with that (we believe in telling employees the truth—or managers might repeat the Cendant crisis on a personal level), but it does underscore how hard the advice is to really follow. The fact that this advice has reinvented some of the greatest careers and companies of all time shows how effective it is. In the end, this decision is up to you.

Great manager-coaches know that there's a way to have people achieve just as much, if not more, and to keep them fulfilled, satisfied, and appreciated at the same time. Great manager-coaches know and live out their own Core Values and teach others around them to do the same.

Escape from Sisyphus's Mountain

For thousands of years, people have struggled with how to achieve their goals without making their lives empty in the process. Plato and Aristotle advocated a reflective life, in which people spend considerable time thinking about their behavior. Throughout the Roman Empire, the usual way to live was for the glory of the Empire—people saw their success as a detail within the greater picture of the Empire. In the Middle Ages, devotion to God was the expected style. In the Renaissance, some people thought that each person has a piece of God in him or her, and should listen to this "inner voice."

We advocate a new approach that is really an old approach reborn. People today often lament the lack of leaders in the world. A recent series of reports on National Public Radio posed the question: Why aren't today's leaders as good as the leaders of the past? They specifically looked at the vast difference in the American presidency since the Founding Fathers.

At the time of the American Revolution, people had a view that each person had a role to play. "All the world's a stage," to quote Shakespeare. Each person's job was to assume a role—such as war hero, leader, or good citizen, and play this role all the time, to the best of their abilities. The thinking was that this role would elevate people above their baser instincts and lead them toward a life of service. George Washington assumed the role of "hero." In one of his first battles, he wrote that the sound of bullets whizzing past him were like music to his ears. Some modern scholars argue that perhaps this role wasn't completely genuine, and that Washington must have felt the terror that any person in this situation would feel.[3] He probably did. So what? His terror wouldn't inspire anyone, and Washington knew that. He also knew what was called for in the moment and what was at stake in terms of the future of the colonies. Washington knew his Core Values and the point is that he played his role so well that people believed his performance enough to brave incredible hardship and risk, and the rest, as they say, is history.

Some people today see a major hole in this thinking: playing a role makes people phony. This thinking takes them off the hook for providing leadership. Leadership is a role position. We see that if the role is followed carefully enough, it will make people more effective in their lives, including in their businesses. We advocate following the wisdom of the ages in this old approach, but with a modern addition that will give it a soul and a heart.

In the 1960s, one of the finest researchers of the century—Milton Rokeach—proposed that people have beliefs, attitudes, and values, and that the human mind seeks harmony between these. He argued that values are specific types of beliefs that are central to the entire mind's system, and they act as life guides in healthy people. If there's a conflict between a value and an attitude, the value usually wins.

So, for example, if a person values freedom, yet believes in communism, he will be conflicted. Rokeach suggested that the value for freedom will usually overpower the belief in communism.

Values are so powerful, Rokeach argued, that even without thinking about it, we're constantly evaluating our behavior against them. The problem Rokeach identified is that we often act without thinking—then feel regret when we see a conflict between what we value and what we have done—like the manager who values worker autonomy, yet yells at employees for not doing the job the way he would have done it.

We take values a step further. We propose that good manager-coaches will help people to identify their own values and then to set goals consistent with these values. Back to Washington.

In his day, there was no coaching process to guide people to a specific role. Thousands died on the battlefield on both sides of the Revolutionary War trying to squeeze into the role of war hero, or patriot, or subject of the king. We believe that understanding and living out Core Values always provides the compass that guides us toward a role that is genuine, and that is, in fact, an expression of our deepest yearnings.

We try to practice what we preach. Dave is the CEO of our consulting company, and John is the Chairman of the Board. Neither of us wanted to assume these roles of prominence, and we only agreed to do it when we defined the roles in a way that fit our values. When we first started meeting to design our partnership, we talked about values a lot. Over the course of a year, we identified hundreds that we liked, but finally settled on only three that we considered to be "core." These values are ethics, fun, and money. In terms of ethics, we wanted our lives—and our business—to always pursue the "noble cause" (even if it costs us in the short term) so that we'll make a positive impact on the business world. We also wanted to have fun in the process, as this is important to us. And, finally, we wanted everything we do to have a positive financial return, a result of influence with integrity. This means that we're running a business, not a nonprofit organization and that we're running it "the right way."

We then picked a person whom we both admire who epitomizes each value. Our view of the noble life was brought to life in the writings of Thomas Jefferson. The cartoon strip *The Far Side*, drawn by Gary Larson, captures our sense of fun and our slightly odd sense of humor. And Adam Smith, the author of the eighteenth-century work, *The Wealth of Nations*, argues for open markets, and he won our prize for influence with integrity leading to financial return. We then named our venture

"Jefferson Larson Smith," after these three people, our role models. JLS Consulting Inc. became the name of our company and we focus on consulting within *Fortune* 500 companies.

While we weren't keen on becoming executives, we were both eager to assume the role that represented a company epitomized by our values. In essence, we "checked in" with our values and created our company in their image. Then we created our roles as executives with these values as our compass.

We never take a consulting job unless it serves the values. Just recently, one of the largest chains of hospitals in the world offered us a long-term contract to help their physicians learn better communication skills. When it became obvious that the people involved were merely looking for a way to *show* that they were dedicated to physician development, and that they didn't really want anything to change, we walked. As Thomas Jefferson would have walked, we believe.

We even set up the company's reporting structure to honor our Larson value. John is the president, who reports to the CEO—Dave. Dave reports to the Chairman—John, who reports to the major shareholders— John and Dave. Any business student who ever passed a basic management class would find this structure odd. We agree. The point is, it works for us.

Our point to you is that your values should determine your role, and that your role should determine your behavior. Once you have "values-behavior alignment," we'll bet you the cost of this book that you'll find greater enjoyment in your work and will produce even more—even though your behavior may not change.

Here's the formula behind what we're arguing. Most people figure out what results they want to achieve, then behave in a way consistent with these results. This pattern looks like this:

Behavior ◀━━ Results

When people only do things to hit a metric, our experience is that they'll burn out very quickly. Their days begin to seem empty, even though they might run around like Martha Stewart on speed. Often they are left with an "is that all there is?" kind of feeling, especially after they have put their heart and soul into accomplishing their goal. Most people can bury their feelings of emptiness for a while, and then it explodes out—sometimes in a "midlife crisis," or a sudden resignation. More often, people get irritable and just start hating life. We think this is not good. There is a better way.

By identifying their values, and then behaving in alignment with them, people experience much greater satisfaction at work and in their lives as a whole. People's values connect to their personal "noble cause." That pattern looks like this:

$$\text{Values} \longrightarrow \text{Behavior} \longrightarrow \text{Results}$$

When your values and behavior are in sync, you can step into the role of a manager-coach who inspires others to do as you've done. While people's behavior may not change in the short term, it likely will in the long term.

We recently coached a senior executive of a sales organization. His concern was that the people under him weren't selling life insurance to their clients. They were selling mutual funds like mad—in fact, they were setting national record sales.

He didn't understand why they weren't selling insurance, even though their commissions were higher on these products than on the mutual funds they kept pushing out the door.

We coached him to coach his employees. He used the "going deep" listening process with them, and something very interesting surfaced: every single person expressed a dedication to *truly* serving their customers. We worked with the executive to help him "see" that they were interested in a noble cause. This was a Core Value.

Another interesting thing surfaced. People didn't want to sell insurance because, to them, only distasteful people sold insurance. "Brown-shoed, door-to-door, wanna-be encyclopedia salesmen," in the words of one employee.

The executive realized that as long as the sales force acted in alignment with their Core Values, they were happy. The executive

coached his sales personnel to "see" that they were in a noble pro-
fession. This was one of their Core Values. This insight alone spurred
greater productivity.

This awareness didn't completely solve the situation, however. Several of the salespeople were known to sell "for the numbers," and when
they hit their targets, they stopped working. They were working for the
results. The executive had to go the extra mile with these members of
his sales staff and coach them to relate to the customer in accordance
with their other Core Value of service rather than chasing a result. After
his coaching session with them, they behaved according to that value,
and this speed bump vanished. Their sales increased. But still, the executive noticed, relatively few life insurance policies were being issued.

After several months, he got his key employees together and used
the "going deep" process to again identify their problem with life insurance. "It's not noble," one of them said after a few minutes of the
exchange.

"Really?" he said. "Have any of your clients died?"

Several heads nodded.

"Well, what did you do?" he asked.

"I sent a card and went to the funeral," one brave soul offered.

"Was that noble?"

"Yes."

"Was he insured?" the executive asked.

"Thank God he was," the broker responded. "And very well, through
his employer."

"Gentlemen," the executive said, looking out at a crowd of all men,
"are all of your clients insured?"

Silence.

"Think of how bad you'd feel if one of them died and wasn't
insured. Sending a card isn't enough. Nobility demands that we knock
off this stuff about brown-shoed salesmen only selling insurance. Getting
all our clients insured isn't just noble, it's the right thing to do."

No one said anything, but a few facial expressions were the equivalent of *duh*. It began to dawn on them that providing insurance products

was a needed and necessary part of helping the customer protect his family in case of death, prepare for retirement, and set up his legacy at the end of a long, successful career.

"Will you do it?" the executive probed.

"That's not what I do well," one of them said. "I don't want them to think that I'm pressing them to get a sale."

"Well, then, how about donating your profits from these sales to charity?" the executive asked. This was a brilliantly provocative question.

"We don't mind it that much," a different person said. Laughter filled the room.

"Will you do it?" the executive asked again.

"Alright, we will," they responded, completing the "say" portion of the coaching process through a declaration of future action.

When the next month's sales report came in from New York, the executive leaned back in his chair and smiled. "I love these guys," he thought, as he read over the "record sales increase" section under "life insurance policies."

Values-Led Work

Legendary ice cream duo Ben and Jerry define their Core Value as social responsibility, which they define as doing good for society and for the environment. This goes beyond good deeds—it permeates many of their company's day-to-day activities, like cherry sauce through Cherry Garcia ice cream. Their values lead their corporate mission statement, operating plan, and business strategy, which are prominently displayed throughout their operations.[4]

In the ice cream business, choosing flavors would be an enviable task for most people. Ben & Jerry's considers this decision to be critical. *Duh.* It must flow from their Core Value of social responsibility. *Aha.* They chose Rainforest Crunch and put it in a forest-designed container that creates awareness of deforestation. *Wow.*

They make a conscious effort to integrate their Core Value with the return on profits to shareholders—and most of the time, these things are not contradictory, at least in the long run. Ben and Jerry write: "Our experience has shown that you don't have to sacrifice social involvement on the altar of maximized profits. One builds on the other. The more we actualize our commitment to social change through our business activities, the more loyal customers we attract and the more profitable we become."

Orientation around the Core Values leads to the behavior that produces the result.

Buzzwords and Catch Phrases

It's easy to beat on a phrase like "Core Values" until it becomes a meaningless buzzword. And since lots of people are talking about Core Values currently, there's a danger that this useful phrase will lose its meaning. It's a trap of virtually every new management technique or communication tool, whether it's used in business or personal relationships. But it's a trap that's easily avoided.

When Core Values are betrayed—when people in positions of power act inconsistently with what they've stated are their Core Values—there's a cost. The people around them lose confidence in their leadership, become cynical, and quality of work soon suffers. This is what happened at Cendant Corporation. At that point, all the talk in the world about Core Values won't do a thing: it will have become a meaningless buzzword.

Many people have to reach this low point before they can turn Core Values into a useful operating tool. But wait! Here's the good news! We've found that not everyone has to hit this low point.

Core Values As a Management Tool

Lots of companies have "Mission Statements" that describe, often in glowing language, what the company will do and how they'll do it.

Many of these statements include a segment on the company's values. Often, these are things like "integrity," "appreciation," "family orientation," "work hard, play hard," and the like.

To be honest, most companies produce these values statements in retreats with senior management. Often, these values reflect a combination of their—and only their—values. Sadly, some executives take a "whatever" attitude toward values, and are more anxious to end the meeting than to produce a working document that could help the company manage.

In any case, the values of the company are not the place for manager-coaches to start. We suggest setting any corporate values to the side when working with your people.

We have two reasons for this. First, values identification is a "bottom-up" activity, meaning that employees need to be involved in the creation of a values statement or it won't represent them. It'll seem like "taxation without representation." Second, employees often become cynical, or even scoff, when these values come up. As one employee of a major defense contractor recently told us, "The values of this place make as much difference to me as what they're serving in the executive dining room."

This level of cynicism is the usual effect when values have been trampled on, or simply ignored. A large HMO published its statement of values, which included putting employees first. The same HMO cut out the employee benefit of paid health club memberships but increased corporate spending for country club memberships for top executives. Maybe the decision-makers had a good reason for doing this. Who knows? However, their actions were widely interpreted by the rank and file employees as saying the Core Values were simply lies.

The place to start, then, is with your employees. "Go deep" in discussions with them to identify clearly their own Core Values. After you've done this with each person, see what values the group has in common. Have them "say" what those values are. Make these the operating team values. Finally, let the team manage itself with the values as a guide.

One team we worked with emphasized "efficiency"—the desire to get their work done "and get out of here," as they put it. Another emphasized "friendship"—they wanted to spend time getting to know each other, even if this meant doing social activities outside of regular work time.

In most cases, you'll find that your team's values are very consistent with the corporate values. In 99 percent of cases, you'll find that the team's values are reflected in at least part of the corporate values. Either way, it's good to "see" whatever alignment you can.

The "Sell Out"

In many companies, the commitment to Core Values goes right out the window as soon as work gets complicated. Managers begin looking for shortcuts to near-term achievement (they push that rock harder), or they violate one or more of the company's stated Core Values in attempting to reach a challenging goal. Environments like this—like Marc's small software company—breed cynicism and distrust. When people see the values they've supported violated repeatedly, they lose faith in their managers, lose confidence in their company, and either leave or quit on the job.

One management myth is to think that it's the employee's job to uphold the Core Values and to behave consistently with them. Effective manager-coaches know that this is backward. In fact, as manager-coaches, the maintenance of Core Values is always our first concern. One company that got it right circulated a memo to the same executives (the founders of the company) who had been instrumental in setting the values, saying that it was their primary job to uphold the values at all times. They went so far as to refer to it as "the prime directive," and that any employee—at any level—puts his or her job in jeopardy by compromising the values just to take a shortcut. This memo had teeth because the executives who received it were the same ones who sent it—as a team effort.

The manager-coach knows that if her usually strong employee begins to trample on a Core Value, it's almost certainly a reaction to

Core Values being undermined higher up in the company. It is obvious to the manager-coach that the employee has evidence of "higher up" violations of the Core Value and thinks his own violation is justified. That manager-coach will sit down with the employee and look to see where the values are under assault. Once she's allowed the employee to put all the "trash" into the "Hefty Bag," the employee can look to see where he has violated his own Core Values.

This brings up a difficult point. This is the case of values being violated by people, usually higher up, over whom they have no control. How does a manager-coach respond? The answer is simple, but somewhat unsatisfying. The satisfying answer is to publicly embarrass them into a public "I have sinned!" routine. We do not recommend this. Even when it succeeds, it fails, because it creates enemies.

We presented this situation to Kevin Cashman, CEO of Leader-Source. Kevin was one of the first people in the country to see the brilliance of the coaching model, and his company continues to develop some of the most innovative coaching practices used in companies today. LeaderSource has been called the "Mayo Clinic of Leadership Development" by Fast Company and enterprises such as 3M.

"I start by thinking about Gandhi," Kevin told us. "What if Gandhi walked into my office and asked for coaching? Would I tell him that the British were violating their own values and that he should just leave? I'd encourage him to stay, to lead by example, and to not give up until people lived their values.

"If our first instinct is to jump ship, this says more about us than about the situation. We should stick around and try to change things.

"As people are coached effectively, their sense of congruence—and the lack of congruence—will increase. They will start to see examples of people not living their values.

"And this is one of the best things that can happen. A perceived lack of congruence gives us our mission. It's what drove Gandhi. I remember my favorite quote from [Warren] Bennis: 'Leaders remind people what's important.'"

We would add that "A coach reminds people of who they are, even when they forget." This line is from Tom Landry, the late coach of the Dallas Cowboys.

Kevin adds: "Our job as coaches is to help them to see it [the lack of congruence between values and action], and then hang in there to transform it. This will give them more passion and courage."

It reminded us of one of our favorite quotes from Goethe: "If we treat people as they are, we make them worse. If we treat them as they ought to be, we help them become what they are capable of becoming."

Core Values As a Recruitment Tool

After you've coached your group into identifying, meshing, and dedicating to their Core Values, you have a remarkable opportunity. At the time of this writing, the job market is starting to crack after being historically tight—unemployment is still near a record low. Many of our clients are asking how to lure employees away from the competition. While we think that this situation is temporary, it does give savvy managers an opportunity to recruit people in a new and ethical way.

At JLS Consulting, we start our meetings with potential employees with the story of how John and Dave spent afternoon after afternoon at a Santa Monica deli discussing values. We show them the values we finally picked, and describe how the company really does try to live up to its values. By the time we're done, people's eyes are usually wide with excitement. As a fairly young company, we often can't match salaries from the more established consulting firms. And we don't have to—many people have turned down "better" offers to come and work with us because they are attracted to our sense of mission. They want to work in a place like ours because we take our values seriously.

You can do the same, but only if you really do use values as a management tool. The key here is to show that you—as the manager-coach—are the chief defender of the values. In wartime vernacular, this is a hill worth dying on. We get a lot of mileage out of our true story about turning down work because we thought it wouldn't be fun, or because it wasn't serving ethical ends.

We encourage managers to rework the team values after a large change in staff. In our company, we revisit our values every six months. Even though we're still dedicated to the same values, the exercise is extremely valuable. We call it "going to church," because it reminds us of what's important to us.

The Joy of Work

A television advertisement features a group of children talking about what they want to do when they grow up. "When I grow up," one boy says, "I want to be under-appreciated." "I want to claw my way up to middle management," says another. A third boy says with a wicked grin, "I want to be forced into early retirement."

The ad is funny because there's a bite to it. In it, we recognize ourselves, and see how far we may have strayed from the kinds of things we dreamed about doing when we were children. Remember? Maybe you wanted to be a firefighter, saving lives and rescuing wayward cats from very tall trees. Or perhaps you wanted to run a company that made products that made people's lives significantly better.

Back then, as children, we were all keenly aware of our Core Values. We knew that we wanted to make an important addition to the lives of our families, our friends, and our communities. We knew that we wanted our work to be fun, too. Now, for many of us, we say that those dreams or those goals "just weren't realistic."

Real business isn't like that, we might say. It's not so altruistic. Real business, some of us now say, is about grinding out the results. It's about pushing a rock up a hill, like Sisyphus.

Manager-coaches know that the people who get the same joy from work that they once dreamed of as children are among the most productive, most loyal employees. They're the ones who make their managers shine in the eyes of *their* bosses. Manager-coaches successfully put their employees back in touch with their own Core Values, and demonstrate how those values fit with the company's Core Values. Where the manager has violated a Core Value and trampled on his employees' trust, he cleans up his act and uses the tools of coaching to restore confidence. The workplace becomes a healthier environment, and cynicism and mistrust all but disappear.

Our suggestion is always to start with your own value assessment. What's important to you? What did you dream about as a child? What values have you lost sight of? We suggest you take a vacation day—or even 10 minutes in the morning for a few days—to identify and recommit to your values. Then "say" those values out loud to someone. Pick someone whom you respect and who will hold you to those values. When you do, you will have taken an enormous step in becoming a leader. As you coach others through this process, you will be playing the role of manager-coach.

chapter eight

Ending the
Griping Epidemic

The world seems to live in fear of epidemics. Recently, the movie *Outbreak* portrayed a disease that would have decimated the population of the world. Even more recently, Tom Clancy's *Rainbow Six* painted the scenario of an engineered variant of the Ebola virus that would have killed off 99 percent of human life.

We don't have to think back to the Black Death to remember epidemics that wiped out entire neighborhoods. In 1918 and 1919, an influenza outbreak killed as many as 40 million people around the world.[1]

Perhaps the fear of epidemics is that the viruses or bacteria are transmitted silently, and that people's only real defense is to cut themselves off from society. Epidemics turn our social nature against us.

This chapter isn't about epidemics, at least in the conventional sense. But it does describe a consequence of our contact with other people. Unlike a viral outbreak, this chapter describes a social epidemic that we choose to join, even though we may not consciously realize the choice.

This epidemic hits at the heart of what makes business work. It can cost individual businesses vast sums of money, often without anyone noticing. It has literally driven many companies out of business. Unlike influenza or Ebola, the toxic symptom of the disease is often hard to recognize. It masquerades as "business as usual," or "the way things are around here."

The disease we're talking about is *jobus non-productivitis*. The symptom is griping. It starts with a common, ordinary complaint. In the moment of the complaint, work slows, or perhaps even stops. A routine trip to the coffee machine or the restroom turns into an extended stay because, simply put, complaints breed and complainers are carriers of the disease.

If you think we're exaggerating, notice the cycle. Someone in a culture lobs in a gripe about something trivial—the coffee. "It tastes like tar," one person says.

"On good days, it tastes like tar," says another. "Most days it's more like sh—."

Everyone laughs.

"You know what else," another person tosses in, "they buy the cheapest coffee machines around. If those machines were SUVs, they'd tip over."

Everyone laughs, this time louder.

"The coffee's nothing compared to the benefits. I feel like all they pay for is third-world medicine. My MD went to school in Haiti." Notice how the gripes go from trivial to serious.

"I hear you," another adds. "They just don't care about us. We're just poorly paid chumps for working here."

"I'm sick and tired of working eight-hour days while Rob [the manager] comes in at ten and leaves at four. You know he gets a better health plan and makes a hell of a lot more than us."

And so it goes. Notice that one tiny gripe—the coffee isn't Starbucks—degenerates to issues of fairness and management competence. Believe it or not, this dialogue is based on actual conversations we've overheard as consultants in one particular company. Most gripes escalate to this level in under a minute. Yet in this minute, people's morale plummets because of the outbreak. When they return to work, productivity drops off a cliff, office theft soars, and mistakes and workplace injuries multiply like acne during puberty. Worst of all, the outbreak is invisible to the managers.

You might be reading this thinking that your department is immune from the outbreak because you spend more on coffee, offer better health benefits, and because you work longer hours than any of your employees.

That's exactly what the manager of this department said when we told him he had a problem. The coffee wasn't Starbucks, but it was more expensive than the coffee most people use in their homes. The coffee machines were rated by Consumer Reports as a "best buy," because they all make about the same coffee and this model was more reliable. The employees were offered their choice of health plans, from basic HMOs through expensive PPOs. Most employees accepted the basic plan. According to an HR survey done a month later, more than 70 percent of employees weren't aware they had a choice. The manager had no idea that this was going on.

As for the manager getting in at 10:00 and leaving by 4:00? He arrived most days at 7:00 and was gone by 7:30 to a re-engineering meeting that was putting together a new business model of the entire enterprise. It was over by 10:00, when he returned to the office. He did leave at 4:00 to attend an evening MBA program, but often came back to work at 9:00 for at least another hour. He was paying for the MBA program himself and came back to work to answer his e-mails and voice mails from employees so they wouldn't have to wait on him.

Anatomy of an Outbreak

So what happened in this example? Why do gripes breed more than compliments?

Griping is not a new phenomenon. As far back as Freud,[2] eminent psychologists have examined why people repeat gripes and why one complaint usually leads to others. There are at least two reasons. First, to disagree with a gripe makes the dissenter seem like someone who's been duped. Agreeing that we're all poorly paid chumps makes us all seem up on the scam—even though it also makes us chumps. Second, a gripe usually is veiled by a kind of dark humor, and that kind of humor leads to more humor. As anyone who's ever gone to a comedy club knows, the early jokes are usually rated PG or even G, while the last comedian of the evening is often an R-rated clone of Andrew Dice Clay. So not only do gripes lead to more gripes, they lead to bolder and more cutting humor, often crossing the line on race, gender, sex, or religion. Put these two reasons together and we see a big payoff for the griper—he seems smart, funny, and wise. In short, he's the leader of a counterculture.[3]

Put this counterculture leader in a team and several things happen. First, no one dares to tell him he's wrong—the person who does seem misinformed, even inept, for not realizing the "obvious" truth that "we're all just slaves to the greedy boss." Second, people try to emulate him. Third, because he's funny, people will try to get him going. In one team we examined (a team with an "ineffective" culture), the goal of just about everybody was to get Donna "on a roll." When she was "on a roll," or "in the zone," she had everyone laughing so hard their stomachs hurt.

Let's back up another step. When a gripe is lobbed into a culture, it causes a feeling of distress and a negative view of the company. These negative feelings cause more gripes, which lower the morale even more. While all this is happening, work virtually stops. And since anyone who disagrees would be seen as either a management plant or just plain stupid, virtually everyone is dominated into "pledging their allegiance" to the gripe cycle and joins in. Those few who decide to remain disease-free usually walk into their office and close the door, or simply shut up. They have effectively severed their informal relationships with their coworkers and are now suspect.

In time, the cost to everyone will become obvious. People are unhappy going to work. While the gripe cycle can be entertaining, it leaves most people feeling either angry or sad. The first signs of a problem—increased errors and rising employee turnover—usually take managers by surprise. By the time it gets to this level, the outbreak is an epidemic—almost everyone is either infected or living in isolation.

Dismantling the Gripe Cycle

At a leading manufacturing company where we've led some training programs, a rising mid-level manager oversaw a manufacturing operation. The department was a mess; people hated their jobs and complained to one another almost constantly. Problems were rampant, and often the entire operation would shut down due to process breakdowns, sometimes for days on end. The manager realized that if things didn't change, and change quickly in his department, not only would his people continue to flounder, his own ascent within the company could end.

So this manager (new in this assignment) took active steps to short-circuit the gripe cycle. Every Friday afternoon, he ended work an hour early and offered an invitation to everyone in the plant to join him for nachos and beer. This wasn't a formal meeting; there were no speeches and no agenda. People were free to come and go as they wished. However, if they didn't attend the nacho party, they were expected to work.

Since people don't want to look dumb by working when there was free beer, most accepted his invitation. As he wandered around and met people, he listened—deeply. Not that he was eavesdropping, but he would hear snippets of conversations around him. Every once in a while, an employee with some backbone would tell him about one of the gripes blazing across the plant.

After each party, he tried to address at least one of the gripes he heard about. One employee told him that the kitchen in one part of the building was cold. He contacted the facilities manager over the weekend, and the two visited that kitchen on Sunday. They both stayed until they were sure the problem was fixed. The next Monday, this manager sent out a memo to the employees of that section reporting that the problem had been fixed. He even thanked the employee who had raised the concern.

In two months' time, the mood of the Friday nacho parties was very different. Employees usually mobbed him, both thanking him for solving problems and telling him about new issues. He created a safe environment for communication and earned their trust—the first step in effective coaching is also the first step in ending the gripe-distress-gripe cycle.

Notice what happened. Instead of wallowing in the gripe, this manager looked for the hidden unmet need or request that lives within each complaint. The employee who said: "It's cold!" *thought* he was asking for the temperature to rise, but the people around him heard it as a gripe—causing more gripes and more distress.

The manager-coach, though, heard the unspoken request, addressed the unmet need and fixed the AC vents. When the manager switched the topic gripe to action, the negative emotions were drained away and his epidemic stopped. By listening, the coach was being coached on what actions to take. Brilliant coaches are also coachable.

Wash Your Hands

Some infectious disease experts argue that the Black Death was eventually stopped by better hygiene efforts—simple bathing and washing. Next time you're in a meeting when someone spreads the gripe virus, here's the equivalent of forcing that person to wash: "I heard your gripe. What's your request?"

In 99 percent of cases, this sentence will kill the epidemic in its tracks. It purges the disparaging complaint and empowers the employee to come up with solutions.

An executive we trained to become a manager-coach was running a meeting of her direct reports when someone said: "We are really underpaid!" Everyone looked at the VP to see how she would respond. "I heard your complaint," she said. "What is your request?"

The manager laughed. "I request that we get paid more."

"You know I can't do that. Can you suggest something I can do?" the VP responded without a second of hesitation.

"I request that we do a salary survey to see how much we're underpaid."

"I'll work with HR to start a salary survey analysis. Now, let's get back to the meeting."

Two months later, the VP received the results of the survey—her people were paid fairly, even overpaid by industry and geographic standards. She reported this finding to all the managers in the meeting. When she passed out a memo summarizing HR's review (with their permission), she had killed that epidemic.

Most gripe epidemics spread throughout an organization in which most managers are unaware of what people think of them.[4] This brings into focus the cost benefit of effective manager-coaches who encourage safe, open communication from their employees. This is vital to any healthy business.

From Gripes to Contracts

As we've seen, work environments infected with chronic complaints run at less than optimal efficiency. They could even be described as sick.[5]

Encouraging employees to "say" their gripes in the form of a request is an important step in the cure of the epidemic, but it's a fateful step. If employees ask for action, and you agree to take it, you must realize that your reputation is on the line.[6] Manager-coaches who agree but don't follow through are called "incompetent," "untrustworthy," even "liars" by some employees.

How, then, do we manage requests? We think of them as "contracts," to emphasize that they must be formally offered and accepted. Breaching one has a serious penalty. While our "contracts" won't hold up in court, manager-coaches use them to kill gripe epidemics and focus on positive action.

When a manager-coach asks an employee to rephrase a gripe as a request, she has to be prepared with a system. Building on Searle's "speech acts,"[7] Fernando Flores[8] proposes a method that has been widely studied in cognitive psychology and computer science.

Our approach—based on Flores's system, Aristotle[9] and John Searle— is to state a formal "yes" or "no" in response to a request, or to propose a compromise. There are really only three possible responses—yes, no, or a move toward compromise. Here's how it can work:

Employee: The work environment is terrible around here. (Gripe)

Manager-coach: I understand your complaint. What's your request?

Employee: I request better working conditions.

Manager-coach: That's too broad. What's a more specific request? (This is a proposal for a compromise.)

Employee: It's too hot. Can we get air conditioning? (A new request)

Manager-coach: I'll bring this up with my director this afternoon. I'll get back with you tomorrow. Is that okay? (A proposal for a compromise)

Employee: Yes.

Manager-coach: Agreed. (Acceptance of "contract")

Notice that this approach takes the manager-coach all the way from a gripe to a "contract." This manager is now on the hook to get an answer to the employee tomorrow, or her reputation and ability to manage in the future will suffer.

One of our clients taught us a lot about the importance of responding to "contracts," even when the circumstances changed. She had agreed to several "contracts" when her father became sick, and eventually died. While she was out of town dealing with this loss, she took five minutes out to call back a new employee to tell him that she was out of town and requested an extension on an agreement they made. The employee agreed immediately on the phone, and told us that he was extremely impressed that she called to *ask* for an extension, rather than to just demand one. When we reported this to her, she said, "We'd made a 'contract.' You can't just break 'contracts' because things happen."

Manager-coaches also use "contracts" to manage the performance of their employees. Here's how that can work:

Manager-coach: I request that you get this project done and delivered to the client by 5:00 P.M. Monday.

Employee: I have a deadline on the Smith account on Monday. How about 5:00 P.M. on Wednesday? (Proposal for a compromise)

Manager-coach: How about Tuesday at 5:00? (Proposal for a compromise)

Employee: I can make that work.

Manager-coach: So we have an agreement—Tuesday at 5:00, is that right?

Employee: Agreed. (Acceptance of "contract")

Notice that this employee felt free to negotiate with his manager, rather than take the path of many employees: say "yes" and then gripe about the workload. This employee felt free to say "no" to a request, and the manager did not feel compelled to accept the objection. In this case, both the employee and the manager feel empowered to work toward solutions that serve everyone.

This example points us back to a lesson from Chapter 1: the importance of creating a safe environment for coaching. Our experience suggests that most employees are afraid to negotiate, so most will take a suggested due date as an edict from pharaoh. Over time, this creates a mutant strain of the gripe epidemic: employees gripe about the unreasonable manager, and the manager gripes about her spineless employees who miss their deadlines.

The Four Boxes of Management

Once employees and managers have agreed to a "contract," there's the matter of following up. Like most subjects in this chapter, following up is one of the most misunderstood and abused tools of supervision.

Simply put, there are managers who always follow up, and there are managers who almost never follow up. We worked with a manager who was an attorney, and believed that follow-up was always a good thing. We can see the limitation of this approach by repeating a phrase from his secretary: "Does this man think I'm an idiot?"

The problem was, she felt that she had earned his trust, and therefore a reduced need for follow-up, but he didn't think of follow-up as having anything to do with trust. It was his job as a manager to follow up, and he believed he was doing his job. He and his secretary were working as well together as a train wreck. He would follow up with his trusted secretary, or a problem employee, in exactly the same way.

As her frustration shows, trust is very important in management. Some employees have earned high trust, others haven't. Those employees who have earned high trust don't need as much follow-up. They need only low involvement. If we put trust alongside involvement in a graph, it would look like this:

High Trust **High Involvement** (A lot of follow-up) This box is perfect for managers who want to frustrate, torture and drive away top talent.	**High Trust** **Low Involvement** (A little bit of follow-up) This box is perfect for employees who have earned trust—it grants them the independence they have earned.
Low Trust **High Involvement** (A lot of follow-up) This box is perfect for employees who are new or not yet proven at a higher level of performance, such as employees recently promoted. It lets them learn with a safety net.	**Low Trust** **Low Involvement** (A little bit of follow-up) This box is perfect for managers who want to go out of business. This is the zone of no management.

Notice that two of the boxes are focused on manager needs, and two put employees first. Sadly, most managers spend their time in either the "high trust, high involvement box" or the "low trust, low involvement box." Managers in the first category are like the attorney we described—they think of follow-up as something they have to do, rather than adjusting for individual needs. Managers in the second category are usually off selling, meeting, or making deals. The Roman Emperor Nero was a perfect example of a "low trust, low involvement" leader. He didn't trust people, he didn't manage people; he fiddled while Rome burned.

The only two productive boxes are "low trust, high involvement" and "high trust, low involvement." When employees are first hired, they aren't proven, and they know they aren't proven. Most of them want follow-up to make sure they're satisfying the requirements while they learn what those requirements are.

If an employee is in this box, ask them what help they need to satisfy the requirements of a "contract." It's as simple as saying: "I'll check in with you on Monday afternoon to see how you're doing." If the employee agrees, you have another "contract"—and again, your reputation is on the line.

After an employee has successfully performed three or four times, he's ready to move to the "high trust, low involvement box." In this zone, no follow-up is necessary until the "contract" is up. If the employee slips, he moves down to the "low trust, high involvement box" until he has recovered your trust—about three or four successes later.

A manager-coach will use the two functional boxes—"low trust, high involvement" and "high trust, low involvement" to help their employees succeed. But there's one more piece of this puzzle: developing employees.

When you listen "for" their Core Values and unrealized potential, you'll probably hear several things the employees aren't currently doing. Administrative assistants may want to become project managers, or managers may want promotion. If you keep them in the "high trust, low involvement zone" forever, you'll probably frustrate them and drive them away.

Encourage them to develop personal initiatives that really stretch them in the direction of realizing their potential and better living their Core Values.[10] Here's a good test of whether the employee is stretching enough: if they don't want your follow-up, it's probably not enough of a stretch. Having people "dive into the deep end" without enough management involvement doesn't empower them, but instead sets them up to fail. In other words, it may teach them that they aren't able to develop their potential, that this whole coaching thing is a sham. In short, it gives them something to complain about.[11] The sequence you want to shoot for is this:

1. Listen "for" the employee's Core Values and unrealized potential. Use the "go deep" listening technique.
2. Tell the employee what Core Values and unrealized potential you heard. If you've given her enough of an insight, you just might get a *wow*. (The "see" step.)
3. Encourage the employee to think of a personal initiative that will stretch her to better live her Core Values and exploit her potential. Many employees will need your ideas and further insight to phrase this initiative. Keep working with the employee until she can phrase this initiative as a personal declaration. (The "say" step.)
4. When you've both agreed to a "contract" that brings that personal initiative to life, offer another "contract" for follow-up. By doing so, you will have put the employee in the "low trust, high involvement" box until they have proven they can succeed at this higher level of performance. (The "do" step.)

You might be thinking what many managers have said to us: "I don't have time for follow-up with the few employees who have proven themselves," or "You're telling me that *all* my employees need follow-up, even those few I count on to do 80 percent of the work?" Actually, that is what we're saying. But your overall workload will actually decrease if you follow this advice. Here's why: as employees develop their skills and realize more of their potential, they get faster at more basic jobs. As salespeople move from selling $100 items to $1,000 items, selling the $100 product becomes easier and easier. So the productivity of the entire team increases. Also, as employees are developing themselves, they'll be more satisfied and won't gripe as much—thus improving productivity.

Positive Griping

So far, we hope we've painted a negative view of gripes, since they can destroy morale so quickly and so decisively. But we don't want to send the message that gripes are always negative. Here's the positive view: in many cases, a gripe contains a valuable piece of information for managers. Managers who hear this information and make changes as a result are better in touch with employees, who are the bridges to customers, suppliers, and other employees.

A classic example is the American automobile industry in the 1970s. According to several accounts of the time, managers had begun to overly rely on what they thought the customer wanted, rather than on what customers really wanted—a quality product. When customers complained about the poor quality, Detroit's response was an arrogant "they don't have a choice." This was true—but not for long.

When Japanese cars first hit the market, their quality made Detroit look great by comparison. Thanks to management geniuses like W. Edwards Deming, and their own drive and ambition, the Japanese learned from each year's mistakes. They did this by listening to the hidden requests inside customer and dealer gripes. Each year they turned out a product incrementally better than the previous year. Before the Japanese competition was taken seriously by Detroit, they were turning out better-built products. Customers, who had been disgusted by the erosion of American quality, bought the imports in such record numbers that Detroit lobbied Washington for tariffs and quotas on imported cars.

The moral of the story is to listen to gripes as if they contain useful information, because they probably do. Remember that great coaches are coachable. Gripes often contain information about what would better serve employees and customers. Using a topic from Chapter 2, you have to listen "for" the hidden request when they come from customers, rather than listen "to" the gripe itself. If you listen "to" the gripe, you'll probably end up defending yourself, which dismisses both the gripe and the hidden request.

As we've seen, many managers don't realize that there is a way out of this difficult, energy-sapping cycle of complaints and distress.

When people complain about working too many hours, or being paid too little, or facing deadlines that seem impossible, what are they asking for? Fewer hours, more pay, and relaxed deadlines? Perhaps, but if this seems too obvious, it probably is. The trick for manager-coaches is to listen beyond the complaint, and to begin to hear the hidden need behind it.

At General Electric, CEO Jack Welch has a "workout program" in place to deal with complaints. Wherever complaints run rampant, or wherever departments get stuck and their results begin slipping, he puts everyone involved in the department together and essentially locks them in a room with the order to "work it out."[12] In these closed-door sessions, all ideas are welcomed, all complaints heard. It's then up to everyone involved to uncover the hidden requests behind the complaints, to negotiate the contracts required to address these requests, and then to fulfill the contracts.

We think this is one of the smart ways to manage people. In this model, complaints become the basis for the kind of directed and targeted action that moves the department, and the company, forward.

Look and see: where has the epidemic of griping seized your organization? Can you spot some of the requests behind the complaints? How will you turn these complaints—your own included—into requests and eventually "contracts" that will move *your* department forward? When you, and others in your department, "say" these requests for action, your entire department will benefit from the coaching process.

part three

Do

"Iron rusts from disuse, stagnant water loses its purity, and in cold weather becomes frozen: even so does inaction sap the vigors of the mind."[1]

Da Vinci's words so eloquently describe how brilliant insights become powerless without action. Old habits will choke the lessons learned in the "see" stage, and the declarations made in the "say" stage, if we do not follow through with the most important part of the formula—"do."

We have reached the point in the book where coaching can get tough, yet where manager-coaches can make the biggest impact. It becomes difficult, because we don't always see results from our efforts—at least not at first.

In the hit Gen X movie, *The Karate Kid*, a young teenage boy wanted to learn karate to defend himself against the school bullies. Yet, his coach saw potential in him that went beyond self-defense. The kid's first practices were a disappointment. In fact, it seemed like his coach was taking advantage of him, having him do chores around his house. But when the coach returned, he proved to the kid that the muscles he had developed by doing these chores gave him the ability to block punches and kicks—the first lessons of self-defense.

The next three chapters go into some of the more grueling parts of coaching. Holding people accountable may be difficult for managers who want to be popular among the employees, yet this makes the difference between talking about Core Values and acting on them. Clearing through the Clutter of delayed decisions is hard work, but it is an investment that will save time and resources in the long run. You will also learn about the J Curve on the path to excellence in the chapter with that title.

chapter nine

Holding People

Accountable

When you're a Japanese automaker and you're not Toyota or Honda, it's certainly challenging to stand out from the crowd.

By the late 1990s, while Japanese vehicles infiltrated the U.S. marketplace, Nissan Motor Corporation had trouble competing. Its cars sold poorly in comparison to competitors like Toyota, and losses in market share escalated quickly. It didn't take long for those market share losses to show up on the bottom line. Even potential partners like Daimler-Chrysler walked away from possible affiliations. But then in early 1999, French automaker Renault bought 37 percent of Nissan, and Renault's executive vice president, Carlos Ghosn, took the driver's seat.

Ghosn identified some key problems, and found a source for many of them. He stated in interviews that no one seemed to feel any sense of responsibility for the brand. And he took this one step further by asking managers across the company to make specific commitments to sales numbers. "People must feel there is nothing guaranteed when you don't deliver," he said.[1]

Whether he designed his program with this intention or not, when he stepped into the office at Nissan, Ghosn brought with him one of the most powerful tools a coach has. He brought an understanding of the difference between responsibility and accountability. Better still, he brought his knowledge that one cannot exist without the other.

So, in his determination to create a corporate culture where people across the organization take responsibility for its success, he's holding people accountable for what they promise to deliver.

Accountability and Responsibility

These two words, "accountability" and "responsibility," get tossed around a lot. In our consulting practice, we hear them all the time. In fact, we sometimes hear them used interchangeably, and we think that's a mistake. It may be a subtle difference, but responsibility and accountability just aren't the same thing.

Responsibility is an obligation that someone "accepts." It can't be delegated or passed on to a subordinate.[2] Once a person accepts responsibility—that is, the individual "sees" what that responsibility is (necessitating a clear job description) and accepts it verbally—she becomes accountable to "do" it. A manager-coach holds this person accountable.

Think about "see, say, do" again. Let's say a manager works with an employee until she "sees" a new or expanded vision of her work. Then that employee makes a statement about it—think back to the chapter on declarations. Now, that manager-coach and employee together are responsible for making that vision real. So, if the manager-coach is really coaching, he'll hold his employee accountable for all of the specific steps and actions necessary to accomplish what she has "seen" and "said." As she meets the targets of her accountability, the employee is both more effective at work, and is more fulfilled as well. And as her ability to meet specific accountabilities improves, she becomes ready to take on larger areas of responsibility and bigger accountabilities.

This is quite straightforward on a personal and individual level. People set a goal and move toward it, either handling their own accountability or working with a coach as they work toward the goal. They reach their goal, set a new one, and move on.

Anyone who has ever worked at a company where employees were neither responsible for some area of success nor accountable for reaching the measures of that success knows that such a company is headed for serious trouble. That should be fairly obvious. What's perhaps more interesting, though, are companies whose employees are dedicated, hard working, and highly accountable, but who still run into difficulty. After all, if an individual can achieve a goal by meeting the measures of accountability, shouldn't it be the same for a corporation?

Cultures and Accountability

There are lots of organizations whose employees fit that description of high accountability. But where the culture fails to gain each and every employee's acceptance of responsibility for something greater than his or her own area of work, problems sometimes result.

In the western United States, the Nordstrom department store expanded from Seattle and became enormously successful on the strength of its reputation for providing sensational customer service. In many cities, the arrival of a Nordstrom store set dedicated shoppers' hearts afire with visions of service so personalized that the salespeople literally carried notebooks in which to keep track of their customers' preferences. Even when the chain reached 22 west coast stores, salespeople still carried those books. In fact, one of our own associates tells us that he often received calls from his "personal sales-guy" at Nordstrom letting him know when new shipments of his favorite shirts had arrived. Clearly, this was an organization where salespeople were highly accountable, and where they were reliably responsible for their area of work. Nordstrom's profits grew by double digits.[3]

Something odd happened, though, when the chain began to expand beyond the west coast. By the time Nordstrom reached 99 stores, sales growth had slowed, profits began to disappoint, and the stock market reflected the trouble as shares dropped in excess of 30 percent from their 1996 highs. What happened?

Some retail experts argue that Nordstrom simply took its eye off of fashion trends, and failed to modernize their customer service methods. Remember those notebooks? Even at 99 stores, salespeople still kept handwritten records of customer preferences.

Problems like a failure to modernize and a failure to keep current with customer preferences might not be the real problems at all. Instead, these might be the symptoms of a bigger, more systemic challenge.

Perhaps the problem is cultural. In this case, there may be plenty of people who are accountable for their own success, and there may be lots of managers who are responsible—and accountable, too—for their department's success. In fact, many of these managers are probably quite skilled at holding their employees to account for their sales numbers. And while that's clearly a worthwhile skill set for a manager to have, this could be a case where it's as much a part of the problem as it is a part of the solution.

Consider that sometimes, senior managers and executives—people who are both responsible and accountable for the success of their organization—think that by ensuring that people are held strictly accountable for their own areas of work, they'll "step-ladder" their way to a successful enterprise. In other words, at every rung up the organizational ladder, people are accountable for the output of the people or departments one rung below. It's a logical progression, isn't it?

There's plenty of accountability in a model like this. In fact, with everyone accountable to the manager a rung above, everything should work perfectly well. So why doesn't it?

Here's one reason. Environments like this will often give rise to cultures that are "useful" at best. Look back at the table of the five cultures in the workplace in Chapter 3. Useful is a good culture, but it isn't the kind of culture in which world-class teams grow and flourish. Why?

Because a culture that rewards people for their own, personal area successes might create a workforce that's highly accountable, but it's not necessarily going to be one where everyone shares a sense of responsibility for the success of the whole team, department, or organization.

Let's look at the five cultures of the workplace, and consider accountability in each.

In *undermining* cultures, there's virtually no accountability at all. Recall the example of the government agency for whom we consulted. There, the employees stood outside their offices, gossiping and worrying over how budget cuts would affect them. Those who took a brighter view, or who sat down to accomplish work, were openly ridiculed. In a culture such as this, no one has a sense of responsibility for the success of the enterprise, and there's no chance to hold people accountable. After all, for folks like this, "life sucks," and in essence, it sucks everywhere. So why bother?

A step up from there, in *ineffective* cultures, there's no accountability, but there is an excuse. During the 1990s, the city of Taipei, Taiwan, built a new commuter train system. Like many massively scaled construction ventures, this one featured numerous contractors all managing huge projects. Trains were built, but there were lots of problems. In 1994 the controversy grew so intense that Taipei's mayor was dumped from office when his opponent, Chen Shui-bian, promised to straighten out the messes. By 1996 Matra, the French contractor who made the trains themselves, pulled out of Taiwan altogether amid finger pointing and countercharges.[4]

Several trains caught fire, and computer failures sometimes stranded trains for 40 minutes or more. Taiwanese officials blamed Matra, saying that the technology they brought to Taiwan was suspect. For its part, Matra claimed it was Taiwan's fault, and that the local government had so badly mismanaged the effort that the project was two years behind schedule, and that Matra had lost millions as a result.

Neither Matra nor Taipei's city leaders were willing to be accountable for what was happening to the subway project. Yet both parties (and quite likely many of the people within each organization) had powerful, logical, good-sense-making excuses. It's Matra's fault; they brought bad technology. It's Taipei's fault; they didn't manage the contractors properly. Like most arguments, these can be made effectively depending on what evidence one presents. But the bottom line is that the trains, at least in 1996, still didn't work very well.

Things get more interesting in *useful* cultures, where the overriding sense is that "I'm great," and where the theme of the culture is personal. Think back to the Nordstrom example. There, in a company where salespeople took great pride in the service they gave to their own customers, their antiquated methods of customer care–those handwritten notes–helped individual salespeople a great deal, but hampered the enterprise as a whole. Salespeople didn't have the success of the entire company at stake, only their own personal achievements.

The difficulty may well be that in "useful" cultures, people in the company lack a shared vision in which everyone has an investment, whether it's emotional, moral, financial, or all of the above.

It's markedly different in *important* cultures, where the sense is that "we're great" and where the theme is one of partnership. Look at a company like SAS Institute, a North Carolina software company with 5,400 employees and a turnover rate that's never been higher than 5 percent. In a business where it's considered gospel that the way to keep employees is to pay significant bonuses, huge salaries, and to give stock options, SAS pays competitive salaries and offers no options. What they do offer, however, are outstanding benefits and, more importantly, a culture where people are treated like adults. For example, David Russo, the head of Human Resources, said the following about the company's policy of unlimited sick days. "If you're out sick for six months, you'll get cards and flowers. If you're out sick for six Mondays in a row, you'll get fired. We expect adult behavior." The expectation of "adult behavior" correlates with the company's decision that it will allow people the freedom to work in a way that best suits them. One manager puts it this way: "Because you're treated well, you treat the company well."[5]

SAS isn't a successful company simply because it has built a gym, or because it launders the employees' gym clothes on site. It's a company that's built on intensive accountability. From his office computer, the CEO can monitor essentially every relevant piece of information about the company: he can see sales and technical support data, for example, and can monitor bug reports relating to new software. Every programmer and tester who works on a product finds his or her name printed in the product manual. Managers work alongside their subordinate employees, writing software code, for example. "At my last job," says one employee, "my manager was just making sure that everything got done." In contrast, says the same employee, "My manager is doing what I'm doing. She's in the trenches." Perhaps most demonstrative of the culture at SAS is the following statement, made by an applications developer: "I know everything I do has an impact on the final product. That gives you a sense of responsibility to get things done right and on time."

Without question, the company's unusual practices and policies have detractors, and there are probably some within the company walls. But on the whole, this is a company that shows evidence of an "important" culture, one where partnership is a palpable experience. When people talk in the halls, they're actually talking about work. Wow. And that culture has a real and measurable impact on the bottom line. SAS Institute has a record of outstanding growth in sales, revenues, and profits. And the especially low turnover—recall that turnover at the company has never been more than 5 percent—saves the company tens of millions of dollars in costs related to hiring and training new employees.

Vital cultures offer an entirely different model of accountability. In vital organizations, people are accountable not just for each other, but for a vision in which they're all invested. Recall the story of the biotechnology company we discussed in Chapter 3. There, scientists weren't accountable merely for developing a new drug. Instead, they shared in the company's vision for a healthier future for everyone. And while many companies have a "mission statement" that's posted on lots of walls and bulletin boards, this company has whole groups of employees who are willing, eager, and proud to be accountable for that mission.

How Coaches Do It

It's worthwhile to understand how the culture of the workplace impacts accountability, but this is only one part of the equation. We're still missing the keys to how a manager-coach holds employees accountable.

In many ways, it's all a manager-coach will ever do. In sports, teams are often led on the field or court not by a coach, but by senior players who've stepped into leadership roles. The coach isn't the field leader of such a team, but he does hold those leading players accountable, and often at a higher standard. How do coaches do this?

They don't accept anything but the promised result. And where the promise hasn't been kept, coaches don't hear the excuses that are offered. Around the best coaches, people won't even offer an excuse. Why bother? It's not relevant.

That's often the problem in business situations. Deadlines get missed, deals fall through, things happen. And then, because everyone's looking, we have to come up with some justification, some explanation for why we didn't hit the target.

In sports, coaches know that the only measure that truly matters is the score at the end of the game. It's a little more complicated in business, because there are so many different ways to score the game. If it's all about the balance sheet, that's one score. If it's all about how people feel about working for company X, then that's another.

Business coaches know that there's a reasoning-loop involved in holding people accountable. In other words, they know that people will be more willing to be accountable for a goal or a project when they've got something worth being held accountable for. When people have a stake in something, they're more willing to sacrifice for its success.

It's an obvious principle and one that's used all over the business world. Ordinarily, though, it's a financial incentive. Companies give stock options to employees, or tie compensation to sales targets or other financial measures. Money, after all, is an easy way to keep score.

It's useful, too. At Hewlett-Packard in 1998, the CEO responded to slower growth, shrinking margins, and higher costs by starting to tie managers' salaries to the performance of their individual units, and his efforts filtered down, as the PC Division's head, Duane Zitzner, began awarding stock options to his managers based on revenue growth and shareholder value. This keeps salespeople from offering too-deep price breaks in an effort to make quota, something that had previously cost the company substantially.[6]

So, one tool that coaches can use in holding people accountable is to make sure that they're invested—that they are stake-holders—in what they're doing. It's easy enough on a sports team, or even in a personal coaching situation, where an individual sets a goal that's of clear importance.

But there's more to coaching than offering financial incentives or refusing to hear excuses or justifications. In fact, what coaches offer is something that can be compared to what a parent of a substance abuser is advised by many counselors to offer—"tough love."

Manager-coaches "call people on it." This is where all the work on "see" and "say" finally rounds the corner and arrives at "do." And often, people who have seen a new vision, and said what they'll accomplish, don't actually do it.

This is where manager-coaches can "do" the most good. People don't typically see beyond their excuses or their justifications. "I would have closed the deal this afternoon, but the client had to go to Japan, and his manager's on the same flight, so I just couldn't get to anyone," and on it goes. There are plenty of people—managers included—who hear all these justifications as the real report. Coaches know that there's only one real report: what's the result. The sale closed, or it didn't.

In some situations, people offer excuses and justifications to defuse what they expect will be their supervisor's heated reaction. Managers who berate people who've missed a targeted accountability aren't doing themselves any favors. Think back to the SAS Institute example, and the wonderful statement about how the company treats people like adults and expects adult behavior in return. Tantrums are hardly adult behavior, and yet we've seen numerous companies where manager flame-outs are all but expected.

Manager-coaches who work with employees through the processes of "see" and "say" know that often, people don't follow through on the things that originated from their own minds. They easily lose touch with their values and even their commitments. Life moves quickly, and it's easy for things to get in the way. So manager-coaches have compassion for that, but they don't compromise their objectivity. They're able to remind their team members of what they've seen, and what they've said. They're able to hear everything that the employees have to say, but good manager-coaches aren't listening to the justifications. Instead, they're looking for an opportunity to remind their employees of what they've seen—the values they've identified and come to share with others—and what they've said, as well.

Manager-coaches hold their employees accountable to "do" it.

chapter ten

Clutter Management

Coauthor Dave Logan sometimes talks about the days when he and his now ex-wife, Susan, were in graduate school. "We could never invite anyone over to our apartment—not that we had the time to entertain guests. The closets were stuffed to the ceiling with dissertation research, empty cardboard boxes, and packaging in case we needed to return a computer. We didn't have enough shelf space for all of our books; as a result, the dining room table and floors were covered with unshelved books and papers. We couldn't eat what was in the refrigerator for fear of food poisoning. It is no exaggeration to say that we kept a turkey in the freezer for five years before we were finally forced to defrost it. We were a couple of Oscar Madisons living together, and it drove us nuts. It's a wonder we could think, let alone write, in that environment.

"It's fair to say that our life—or at least our home—was somewhat Cluttered. Perhaps we could have invented a system to deal with it, or gone out and bought some books about how to get organized, or how to make a small space bigger. Maybe hiring a feng shui expert would have helped, but that wasn't quite so popular back then. Regardless, we worked away, finished our degrees, and one evening we had a nice, if slightly freezer-burnt, turkey dinner," Dave said.

Lots of busy people live this way. And here's the myth—the busier people are (that is, the more they "do"), the more clutter they have. From our observations, the opposite is true. The people who manage their clutter are able to "do" a lot more.

A subversive army lurks in America's businesses. This army has damaged numerous companies, and destroyed no small number outright. But it's an elusive army, a wary, clever foe that has learned to hide in plain sight. This evil, destructive force is known by a simple, everyday word: Clutter.

Doug was a brilliant strategist and outstanding manager who ran his own small advertising agency. He really liked Sandy, who showed promise, fearlessness, talent, and was super easy to get along with. Clients liked her, and so did everyone around the office—except when she made a mess of things. As much as Doug liked her, he wished he could rely on her, but he knew that wasn't always possible. She could never be a partner, because he couldn't trust her to think things through clearly. Sometimes she was brilliant, but sometimes just wasn't enough.

Sandy had a lot on her plate—and it was all business she brought into the company, but it began to pile up. The growing stacks of paper that had taken root on her desk overwhelmed her. She started misplacing things—pieces of paper, her to-do lists, approvals from clients, invoices from vendors. They were around somewhere; she knew she would never throw anything important away. To-be-filed piles were mounting toward the heavens like the Tower of Babel.

As likable as she was, she caused real problems for Doug and the people around her. Nancy had to field threatening calls from vendors. Christopher had to re-key lost information. Even Doug was beginning to get a short fuse.

Yet when she was on, her designs were beautiful and made the agency look really, really good. Sandy had spent weeks building a portfolio to take around to clients. Doug wanted her to bring it to an awards dinner. He only mentioned it to Sandy once, when she was working on it. He didn't think to mention it again, because she seemed excited by the idea.

At the banquet, Sandy and Doug met several people who were interested in their services. Doug sent people over to Sandy to look at her portfolio. But Sandy forgot to bring it. She didn't mention it to Doug that evening because she forgot that she forgot.

"You forgot?" was Doug's shocked response.

"Doug, I'm sorry. If it was that important, you should have reminded me."

"Excuse me? I should have reminded you? Try again, Sandy. Once I tell you something, it's out of my mind. You should have written it down."

Doug salvaged the situation by following up with all the contacts he had made, but he was tired of salvaging things. The final straw was the lawsuit from an unpaid vendor. Doug finally fired Sandy.

In the final analysis, it didn't matter that Doug liked Sandy's work or that she was talented. What mattered was what she was able to do. Sandy was chronically ineffective.

This story illustrates a principle from coaching. Our ability to "do" things will be hampered by the Clutter around us. This is such a big problem that we're devoting this chapter to it. As a manager-coach, you need your physical space to be clean and efficient or you'll have trouble focusing on the needs of your employees. And the more you help them to "see" that an organized space will increase their effectiveness, the more they'll be able to "do."

Every one of us gets invaded by Clutter. Really, though, it's not so much that we "get invaded." Instead, we "join forces" with Clutter's evil empire, speeding the army's entry through the gates of our company, our department, and right into our offices. That's the way this army works, and how it "hides in plain sight." Clutter makes co-conspirators of us all, from time to time. For some people, Clutter seems to be a way of life. You've seen your colleagues' desks. And they've seen yours. So everybody knows where everyone stands, or so it might seem.

Robin was often embarrassed by the disorganization of her office. On occasion a *Wall Street Journal* reporter called to ask for current product specifications, and after shuffling through the mountains of papers on her desk for the next two minutes, she told the reporter she'd have to call her back. The call was just another thing to add to her growing to-do list, which incidentally was buried under another pile. It was predictable that she would lose the name and phone number of the reporter.

It was a familiar pattern for the busy news bureau. If only there was time to set up a filing system so they'd be ready when reporters called. It would have been a great project for an intern, but Robin didn't have time to find or train anyone. She needed her assistant's help, but she didn't have time to explain how she wanted it done. Plus she felt guilty every time she gave Jody another project to do. The incessant complaining, "I already have too much to do," only gave Robin a migraine.

Once Robin got a migraine, she was shot for at least two hours until she got rid of the pain. She would have loved to fire that assistant, but then when would she have time to find someone else? Besides, at least Jody knew where everything was. They both scurried through the piles to find the specs for the *Wall Street Journal*. When at last they gave up, Robin reluctantly called the product development department and asked for more specs.

"I thought your team got a copy already."

"Yeah, well," Robin laughed nervously, "you know how busy we are over here with the phones ringing off the hook."

"Yeah, but you guys need to get organized."

Well *duh*, Robin thought.

It is a common picture: already overworked employees double-up on job functions. Invoices pile up because no one thinks it's their job to process them, and actual work is usually reserved for after hours when the phones go over to the answering service.

It might seem simple to fix Clutter. Just come in on a weekend and spend it filing and developing a system that can organize itself. Then, when the phones ring off the hook, it will only take seconds to find what you need. Right?

Yet if it's so easy, why are so many departments in the state of hell we just described?

Simple. People think that Clutter is a time problem, and they're wrong. Look at Robin, above. She's pressed to the limit at work: phones ring constantly, people need information immediately. Robin doesn't trust her assistant to perform tasks without thorough instruction but can't or won't spend time giving the instructions.

Time isn't Robin's problem in the example, however. Robin put her department in the control of the Clutter army long ago, when she started putting off decisions. As soon as Robin started leaving one thing undecided in order to attend to an issue that may have seemed more pressing, she opened the door for Clutter's army to march in. Her desk might have been quite clean at the time. But already, Robin had Clutter on her mind. And she had Clutter *in* her mind, more importantly. Eventually, the deferred decisions, and the mental action not taken showed up on Robin's desk in the form of those teetering piles.

Plenty of people can manage their lives and jobs with a certain amount of mental Clutter: Ben might be worried about his persimmon tree, his mortgage, or his son's latest collegiate experiment in the effects of alcohol, but he might also have a high level of skill at setting aside this Clutter to concentrate on his work. Perhaps Ben can also prioritize his tasks amazingly well without using any tools other than his mind. Maybe he can let a few things slip for a time and catch them up later, without any apparent system at all. But even if Ben is exceptionally skilled at ignoring his mental Clutter or "compartmentalizing" it in order to concentrate, if that Clutter surpasses a threshold, it will make itself visible, and fast.

In Robin's example, mental Clutter made its way into physical form in the shape of an office in disarray as well as a harried, frenzied experience for her and her colleagues at work. Chances are, if Robin and her coworkers came in on a weekend and spent a couple days filing papers and organizing desks, they would be okay for a short while. Soon, however, the army would return, and Robin would see what we see now: the Clutter in her office is a symptom, not the problem itself.

If we dropped a manager-coach into Robin's office at the peak of its disarray, it probably wouldn't take long for Robin to see that her office isn't the only part of her life suffering from Clutter. The manager-coach might also show Robin how she has taken Clutter from higher up in the organization, expanded it, and passed it on to the people around and below her in the corporate hierarchy. After all, like gossip, Clutter breeds. A coach could show Robin how she has created an environment that favors Clutter, and how to clean it up effectively—not by treating the Clutter itself (well, the truth is that someone is going to *have* to file all that crap) but by dealing with the underlying condition, and by empowering Robin to make better decisions, faster, and to trust in these decisions consistently and confidently.

What a coach would show Robin is how the army of Clutter is so brilliantly organized. General Clutter works with Major Clutter, right alongside Private Clutter, and all three do the dirty work together. Let's meet the insurgents, shall we?

Private Clutter

Private Clutter musters into the insurgent army alongside every single one of us (including that man reading over your shoulder on the subway right now), almost every single day. Private Clutter consists of all those bits and pieces of life and work that can sneak up and derail us individually. Sometimes these individual items of Clutter are directly work related, sometimes not. It's not hard to see that if Tony is worried about his spiraling credit card debt, he's going to have a hard time concentrating at the office. Similarly, if Tony has a conflict with a coworker and doesn't resolve it, the "residue" of that unresolved problem will undermine both Tony and his fellow worker. Private Clutter hampers people at an individual level. More importantly in terms of organizations, Private Clutter undercuts people's ability to function as part of a team.

We discussed the problem of Clutter with Thomas Leonard, the founder of Coach University and author of *The Portable Coach*. "People's lives can easily gather deferred decisions and things that need attention.

Eventually the echo of these is deafening," he told us. "Then you can't hear your inner voice that tells you what's really important to you."

Thomas advises people in organizations to perform a "clean sweep" (a process he writes about in his book). "The CleanSweep program is a 100-item process that will address life's debris in all areas—health, physical environment, relationships, money, well-being, and so on."

We've noticed that the "useful" items in business—expense reports, memos, voice mail, e-mail—will drown out the "important" and the "vital" elements. The vital elements—those tasks that give us energy, that feed our creativity—are overwhelmed by anything below "vital" on the cultural map—undermining (issues about gossip or backstabbing), ineffective (areas of work and life where we feel like victims), useful (issues dealing with personal competence and effectiveness), and important (items that deal with the competence and effectiveness of most teams).

Building on Thomas' comment about Clutter, we believe that the vital issues only emerge when we clear out the less-important Clutter.

Since we do a lot of writing (a vital task for us—one that makes us feel alive), we've noticed that our writing is poor unless our physical space is clean, our employees' issues are dealt with, our personal lives are in order. We feel a burst of energy when these things are handled and can focus on the "vital."

The good news is that manager-coaches can often intervene quite easily in areas where Private Clutter has begun to gain ground. Generally, a coach's clients can see how they are personally responsible for the Clutter they have allowed to mount around them. And generally, it's a fairly straightforward coaching situation: a manager-coach offers compassionate support within the confines of a contract, in which there's an agreement to clean up the Clutter by a specific time. Simple.

Major Clutter

Major Clutter consists of all those put-off, piling-up, scattered problems that can undermine your team or department. Robin's story provides plenty of examples of Major Clutter: Robin would like to rely on her assistant, but can't or won't take the time to explain tasks fully. Jody, the assistant, is disempowered, Robin is left feeling more deeply over-whelmed, and the entire department loses more of its efficiency and productive edge.

There's no rule against fraternization in Clutter's subversive army. Major Clutter and Private Clutter happily exist side by side. While Robin complains of too little time and too little support from her staff, people like Jody develop Private Clutter of their own: Jody might well resent Robin, further debilitating her own performance at work. Who wants to put out a great effort for someone who is unappreciative, or who openly fails to trust? Why bother? More importantly in this example, why would Jody make the extra effort to move Robin and her department into a new level of organization and fluid management of all their complex, shifting priorities?

Major Clutter—those unfulfilled promises or deferred decisions that affect a close-working team of people—is especially insidious because it builds quickly upon itself, and because it affects an entire team of people. Everyone touched by Major Clutter will have his or her own individual reaction. Some people on a team will bear down and work harder. Others will give up and become cynical. Still others will simply look for another job. Regardless, Major Clutter is a serious threat to the very notion of teams working together.

General Clutter

Great military generals know how to take a systemic, or strategic view, and break it down into tactical action. In business, General Clutter leads his subversive army into the hallways every day from a similar point of view. In our terms, General Clutter is the result of deferred decisions that affect the entire organization. They may not be the result of a CEO or COO's unwillingness to move in one direction or another. But these problems have a system-wide presence as well as an effect on individual members of the organization. Accounting problems at Cendant Corporation are an example of General Clutter: One of the things attributed to Cendant's accounting fiasco is the size of its board of directors—which incidentally made *BusinessWeek's* worst board list.[1] With 28 members, Cendant's board is too big—in fact, twice as big as boards of other public companies—and split down the middle when it comes to making decisions.[2] Hmmm.

Private Clutter, Major Clutter, and General Clutter. The three "ranks" of the subversive army are out there, stalking the hallways of virtually every enterprise. They're chameleons, too: Clutter takes different forms in virtually every organization, amidst every team, and with every individual. One might think that this would make Clutter a tougher foe. Manager-coaches know, however, that Clutter is vulnerable. Even though Clutter is a resilient enemy, it is not that hard to keep beating it back out the door.

The Magic of Action

We have made an officially big deal out of Clutter arising as the result of deferred decisions. But what does that mean in the "real world?" Simple: When people don't decide, they don't act. Unfortunately, in business and in life, when we don't act, things happen anyway. We have to "do" things as they come at us or we defer action, and we accumulate Clutter.

In the world of physics, we learn that a body at rest tends to remain at rest. That's the first part of the law of inertia. We all know, however, that life and business aren't "bodies" that remain at rest. Things happen all the time. We're constantly moving from task to task, "putting out fires," as some of us like to say. Stuff happens. And stuff keeps happening. The second part of the law of inertia states that a body in motion tends to remain in motion (commonly called momentum); this clearly applies to business and life, too. There's a strange confluence of these two principles, however, when it comes to Clutter. Where "inertia," the growing, expanding residue of our nonaction, meets "momentum," the increasing speed and movement of the business that surrounds us, the result is chaos, or what we call Clutter.

Clutter builds because someone, somewhere, has failed to act—or "do." The greater the imbalance between the "inertia" of decisions unmade and the "momentum" of forward-moving business demands, the more noticeably the Clutter will build, and the more intensely its effects will be felt.

Manager-coaches understand that the simple cure for Clutter is to get into action. Deal with it. This seems especially simple and straightforward in the case of Private Clutter, and this is perhaps the easiest part of dealing with Clutter. People can easily be led to see that they, themselves, are responsible for their own Clutter, and it isn't difficult to manage them to clean it up.

The "officers" are a little tougher. With Major and General Clutter, individuals often have a difficult time seeing how they are personally or individually responsible for the problems. "If sales had its specs right, then we wouldn't have to recut all these dies for the client." "If the CEO would just make up his mind about what kind of financing to pursue, then we could finish our marketing plan, hire the right people, and start making things happen." The trouble in these cases is that it's a heck of a lot easier to blame someone else than to look at how we might have an impact in dealing with the problem now. That's the trick in dealing with team- or organization-level Clutter. Great coaches find ways to have their clients "see" how they are responsible for their state of Clutter, "say" what or how they, themselves, can clean it up, and then "do" the actions that will impact that state of Clutter.

Sometimes, we're forced into action, either by impending or actual full-blown crisis. Financial crisis, for example, makes it easy for us to make decisions. T.J. Dermot Dunphy, CEO of Sealed Air Corporation, wrote that debt obligations lead to disciplined management decisions. He was putting a positive spin on how Formica Corporation actually improved while in the throes of a leveraged buyout.[3]

There is something about debt that focuses, or "unClutters," one's decision-making. Not that we recommend getting into it, but suddenly you're having to cease expenses and concentrate your resources on activities that bring in income, if you want to survive.

Impending crisis led Archie W. Dunham, Conoco Inc. chairman and CEO, to make what might seem like an unorthodox decision when oil prices fell. In this time of financial uncertainty, Dunham approved a comprehensive leadership-development program for his executives.[4] He made a decision—without regret—to invest in his people for his company's long-term success. Right or wrong—we can't always tell. But imagine if he had put off the decision.

In these examples, business leaders acted decisively and saw rewards as a result. As we stated, however, what if these kinds of clear decisions could be made when times are good? Manager-coaches put their people in situations where clear decision-making and action are the themes of the day, every day. And they do this especially well where Clutter is just beginning to build, before it can get a strong foothold.

A Call for Toughness

Clutter is a tough, elusive, insidious, resilient, dangerous foe. It takes a tough approach to beat back a tough opponent. Manager-coaches must take a hard line if they are to win not just individual battles against Clutter, but in fact win the long war.

We would never suggest that managers should be cruel, that they should threaten their employees, or that they should mete out justice like some Babylonian king. Much as we admire Hammurabi's efforts in creating civilization, frankly, we find some of his punishments a mite harsh.

In dealing with Clutter, however, manager-coaches must become adept at holding people accountable for cleaning it up. There's a time for compassionate listening, and there clearly are times when it's appropriate to be gentle with employees. This, however, is something else entirely.

We recommend that manager-coaches take a "holistic" or systemwide approach to dealing with Clutter. Where Clutter has taken hold in a coach's department, she might call her team together for a Witches' Brew session, for example, as described in Chapter 12. Here's a good technique:

Have everyone write down five examples of "Private Clutter." These can be anything. Then ask the question: "By when will you clean each of these up?" Now, do the same with "Major Clutter." Again, the question: "By when will you clean each of these up?" Lastly, do the same with "General Clutter." Spend some time with individual members of the team, and brainstorm it. You may be a sensational coach, but you may also be surprised to find that other members of your team spot Clutter where you don't.

As people discover ways in which they can claim responsibility for cleaning up not just their own Private Clutter, but also the problems that affect their team and the entire organization, they are empowered. As we have stated repeatedly, it's a basic human drive to want to make an impact. Coaches know this, and they know how to get out of people's way to *let* them make a difference. Dealing with Clutter is one such area.

It then becomes critical to hold people to account for what they said they would accomplish. Extract promises and back them up with specific and realistic "by when" deadlines. Where the Clutter is most massive, break the cleanup job into pieces—"markers" or "milestones"— and manage people within those deadlines. Make contracts with people, and then fulfill your own end of the contract. They will, too.

As you look around, if you see any Private Clutter, Major Clutter, or General Clutter, it's time to "see" how your effectiveness would increase if you dealt with it. "Say" what you will do, when you will do it, and have someone hold you accountable for "doing" these steps. Then you'll be more empowered to focus on the vital issues. As you do, you'll become a stronger manager-coach.

chapter eleven

The J Curve

And now for the bad news. Things get worse before they get better. The more potential you're trying to release in an employee, the worse they'll become before you see the gains of your (and her) work.

If you've ever worked with a coach for any sport or physical activity, you know this pattern already. Dave tells us the agony of trying to master his tennis serve. "I was a pretty good tennis player in college—I could land a serve in just the right spot nine times out of ten, but my serve had no power. So I started working with a coach. The first thing the coach did was to "deconstruct" my serve into its parts—every hand motion, every slight shifting of my balance. I worked and worked on each part of the serve separately until the coach said I was ready. Then I tried to serve. In ten practice sessions, each lasting 45 minutes, I only landed three serves. And they didn't have the power I used to have.

"I was panicked. I thought I was working with a sham coach, and I tried to undo his coaching. But I found that I couldn't even serve the old way. I had become an incompetent player. I told him about my concern, and he coolly replied: 'Trust your coach.' I didn't.

"He saw the look of skepticism in my face and then drew a letter J in the air. He said: 'We're upsetting the balance of your old serve. At first, you'll get worse. But the payoff is that you'll eventually get much better. Right now, you're in the bummer zone.' After several more weeks of practicing his new techniques, almost magically, my ability to target a serve returned. And as I continued to apply his advice, the power of my serve increased."

This is called the "J Curve phenomenon," because performance follows the arc of the letter J downward before it levels off, then starts to improve. After significant work, your performance is back to the same level it was when you started. But if you keep up the work, your performance eventually surpasses the old level.

It's Like Yellow VW Bugs

Most people have experienced the "Yellow VW Bug Syndrome." You see a few of them on a particular day, and then, as you start looking for them, they seem to be everywhere. It's very useful for manager-coaches to "see" how universal the J Curve is. It will help you motivate and counsel employees as they move through the "bummer zone" of increased work but reduced performance.

The thread of the J Curve runs throughout the social sciences. Economists studying governmental intervention in markets first noticed this phenomenon. At first, researchers noticed that the interventions would often result in the opposite of what they hoped for. But over time, this "backlash" would reverse and their interventions would often have the desired effect.

The same thing happens in our lives. Psychologists from the behavioral, cognitive, and psychoanalytic tradition have noticed that a breakdown often comes before a breakthrough. The alcoholic who stops drinking will act less functional—for a while—before getting better. The person in a bad marriage will get frustrated and depressed after leaving the marriage before starting to feel better.

What You Don't Know Can Hurt You

When the Soviet Union dismantled communism and started to implement free market reforms, the economy got worse—a lot worse, in fact. People realized things had gotten worse, but they didn't realize they were in the trough of the "bummer zone," as Dave's tennis coach called it.

People who don't understand the J Curve will almost never make dramatic and effective changes in their lives—including the one-third of their lives they spend at work. The Russian people, without understanding the J Curve, saw the declines in prosperity as a reason to abort market reforms. As a result of the halfhearted reform effort, the country is locked in an economic depression so deep it threatens the stability of the region.

Being good capitalists, our hope is that a political figure will emerge in Russia and help the people "see" where they are on the J Curve, and that real improvements are only going to come through moving forward. Otherwise, the country may be stuck in the "bummer zone" for a long time. Some political economists even believe that staying in the "bummer zone" too long might cause a civil war.

When Franklin Roosevelt implemented reforms to the U.S. economy in the 1930s, our economy got worse—at first. Then, slowly, things improved, until World War II increased demand and boosted the economy out of the depression.

On a lighter note, many people fudge their way through their first workouts in a gym, often with the help of a friend who knows little more than they do. Eventually, they become good amateurs. Then they invest in a personal trainer, and often feel they have no muscle tone whatsoever—they're in the "bummer zone."

If you take a class in a subject you know reasonably well (but weren't an expert in), you often go through a stage of feeling like you don't know anything about the topic. This is especially true when you're trying to build skills—such as math (at the lower levels), science, physical education, and communication. Many people who drop out of school do so because they experience so many "bummer zones" at once, especially in the first two years of college when people are taking their general education courses.

Once you understand the J Curve, you'll see it everywhere—in politics, in economics, in the people around you, in your own ability to play sports or get in shape. It's one of the most useful insights, we believe, because it will cause you to "see" how improvement really happens. And when you "see" it, you can help those you coach to "see" it, as well.

The J Curve and Coaching

There are two types of coaching—the kind that involves new approaches and the kind that refines old strategies. When coaching focuses on existing strategies that people already use effectively, the J Curve may flatten out—almost to become a reversed L shape.

But as you start coaching your employees to adopt new approaches—like helping the introvert to "see" that she would be more effective by starting to network—it's vital that you and the person understand that a J Curve will result. If the people you coach are normal (as opposed to the rare people who *enjoy* performance dips—who are probably either locked up or wondering why they aren't working), this will bother them—and it might bother other people, like customers. It might even bother people so much that they'll abort the coaching and try to back themselves out of the "bummer zone," which won't work.

Our general rule is *not* to start coaching by telling people about the J Curve. If they believe that things will initially get worse, this belief can turn into a self-fulfilling prophecy and amplify the depths of the trough. Initially, people will expect their performance to increase, and their problems to go away fairly quickly. They'll expect linear improvement, like in chart 2.0.

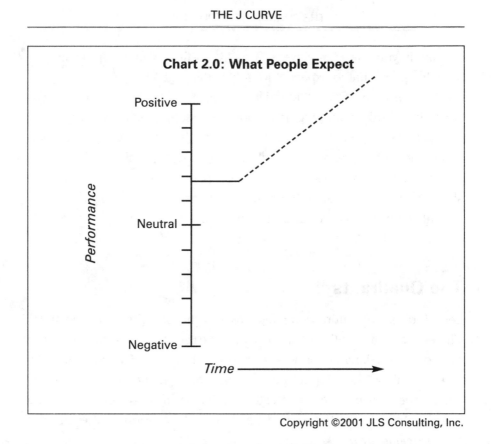

Chart 2.0: What People Expect

Performance (vertical axis): Positive, Neutral, Negative

Time (horizontal axis) →

People expect their performance to improve immediately and consistently. Unfortunately, this rarely happens to anyone in any field.

When people begin to notice that all is not well, presenting the J Curve will often help them to "see" what's really happening, and will motivate them to "stay the course," as Ronald Reagan used to say.

This advice is controversial, and we want to give you the upside and downside about when to present this to people. If you follow our general rule, people might feel like you've taught them to believe in Santa Claus (immediate improvement) and then stolen Christmas from them (by showing them how improvement really works). In the short term, it can damage trust. On the upside, they'll probably start implementing your coaching and, by the time they discover that things haven't gone as they expected, they'll be through most of the "bummer zone."

Yet if you have employees who you think would appreciate the knowledge of what to expect before they start, then it's probably a good idea to tell them. So our ultimate advice is to really think it through yourself and trust your judgment about the people you're working with.

Our best experiences have been when we saved the J Curve for a celebration of success that wouldn't have been possible without the coaching. Then, as a way to review what people have gone through, we show them where they've been, and that they're now in a position to capitalize on the hard work of moving through the "bummer zone."

The Quadrants

Let's look at the entire coaching process through the "lens" of the J Curve. It all starts with the atmosphere of trust you establish, leading to the person's talking about what's important to her—her Core Values. As you "listen for" her unrealized potential, and tell her what you hear, she'll "see" her potential and catch a glimpse of what her job and life could be like if oriented around her Core Values. You might even hear a *duh* or *aha* or *wow*.

The next step is to work with her until she "says" what changes she'll make to realize the potential. Then she'll start to "do" what it takes, and you'll hold her accountable (in a safe way) for taking these steps.

Welcome to the quadrants. As your employees move through the change process, they'll move through all three quadrants—unless they make a decision that aborts the progress.

Each quadrant starts and ends with a decision point. At each point, there are only two choices—to continue along the map of change or to stop. At any point along the J Curve, the decision to stop means that performance development will "flatline." Chart 2.1 shows the quadrants.

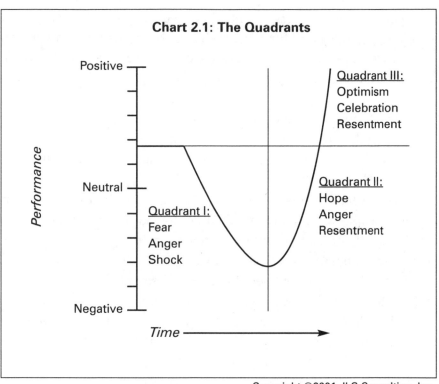

Chart 2.1: The Quadrants

Quadrant III:
Optimism
Celebration
Resentment

Quadrant II:
Hope
Anger
Resentment

Quadrant I:
Fear
Anger
Shock

Positive

Neutral

Negative

Performance

Time

As people start to implement coaching, things may get worse at first, but eventually, their performance will drastically exceed their starting point.

One of our clients—an executive in a large university—once stood before his 50 senior managers and announced that communicating with each other was no longer optional. It was required. He explained what types of interaction he expected and how he would measure whether it really happened. His main measuring tool, he explained, would be whether the senior managers knew what was going on in each of the other divisions.

A month later, he got his senior managers together and began asking each one, in front of the group, to give a report about what was happening in different departments. To his surprise, people seemed less informed than they had been before his announcement the month earlier. He asked us what happened (a good rule for coaches, by the way). We admitted we didn't know and began to ask some questions of the managers.

The managers reported that they were communicating less than they were a month earlier. When we asked them why, they used lots of different words to say what one woman said more eloquently than the others: "We're a stubborn group."

The executive's worst fears came true—his edict had not just been ignored; people were doing the opposite of what he called for. At first we thought that people were in a performance trough. But the truth is that the people hadn't even taken the first step.

This highlights the first decision point—whether to begin the process or just "blow it off." Speaking honestly, most people greet change with skepticism. At Harley Davidson, employees call each new change campaign an "AFP"—"another fine program."[1] It's a subtle way of saying it won't work, so it's better not to begin.

In coaching employees, we strongly urge against rah-rah, motivational, pick-yourself-up-by-your-bootstrap speeches only to send them over the cliff into the "bummer zone." Instead, we suggest working with the person until he "sees" his own unrealized potential. For most people, this draw is so strong it will pull them into changing. No pushing necessary.

Once in Quadrant 1, expect unpleasant reactions to the performance drop. Fear, anger, and shock are common. Programs to initiate change, and the resulting J Curve, are strong—so strong that they have produced workplace violence.

Quadrant 1 Coaching Tip: The Boiling Kettle

While most people won't show up to work with an Uzi (thankfully), they will have strong feelings about what's happening. We recommend the "boiling kettle" coaching technique. To use this technique, first get the employee's permission to have a serious chat about what's happening. Then ask a question to get him talking—something like "How's it going?" As he talks, listen for his concerns. Focus on what he's saying, not on whether you agree or disagree.

As each concern comes up, echo it back in your words. "I understand you feel . . . " is a good way to start. When he shows you that you've gotten it right, restate the need for change, briefly and to the point. Don't contradict his feeling, just restate it. An executive we worked with in space electronics used the "boiling kettle" technique as a basis for an "all-hands" speech. With his permission, we're including a paragraph of it:

"I know there are a lot of emotions out there, and I know they're strong. I've heard people say the change is too hard. I've heard people say we're not getting paid enough. I've heard people say we don't even know if this [re-engineering program] will work. I agree with those concerns. I've felt them myself. When I took over the helm of this division, you know—as I did—that we weren't making money. We had two choices—to put ourselves on the market or change. We all chose to change. Today, we're in the trough of the change process. Let me remind us all—myself included, because I need a lot of reminding—that this was the only option open to us, other than to go to [our parent company] and say we've failed."

At the end of Quadrant 1—which one of our clients calls "the valley of the shadow of death"—there's another choice point. It's the point at which things begin to turn around when there are signs of improvement. Many people at this stage decide to stop the process of change. Tragically, this decision freezes performance at the lowest possible point.

The same client reached this point nine months after a divisionwide change process. During the nine months, return on net assets (the main number the company used to judge its performance) declined to levels so far below the industry standard that the executive had to write weekly memos on why it was happening.

As soon as the change process began to take root, return on net assets picked up. It was still far below the industry average, but several key senior managers decided that "we have changed enough" (as they said in a meeting). The lack of decline was evidence that things will pick up on their own, they reasoned.

Sadly, this is rarely the case, even though this line of reasoning seems to make sense. Welcome to the second decision point. We advise revealing the J Curve to everyone at this point, whether they've seen it before or not. It is a powerful reinforcement that things are going just as planned.

Our other piece of advice is to work with people at this decision point to help them stay focused on the goal—having full alignment with a Core Value and the unlocked potential. In the case of this client, the value was profitability, and the unlocked potential was a company that could win bids outside defense spending by the U.S. government. These pulls were strong enough to keep everyone on track, with the exception of two senior managers who resigned at this point. See you around. Have a great life.

As Quadrant 2 begins, you and your employees will be faced with a new set of concerns. "Why was all this necessary?" they (or you) might ask. It's common for a sense of hope to mix with disillusionment as Quadrant 2 starts.

Quadrant 2 Coaching Tip: Symbolic Celebrations

As Quadrant 2 begins, the boiling kettle technique won't work anymore. People's patience wears out, and "stay the course" often rings hollow.

During this stage, we suggest picking out the small performance increases that result, and celebrate them. American Express is well known for "symbolic gifts" to clients—flowers or a card from a representative if the company didn't serve its clients as well as it should have. We recommend "symbolic celebrations."

The celebration is not a bonus, or recognition in the formal sense. It is a minor way of saying congratulations, from person to person. It should be used informally and infrequently, so that it doesn't become an expectation (and lose its significance).

Bob Reilly, then senior vice president of American Isuzu Motors, wanted his company to sell 10,000 trucks a month. To show his desire to hit this goal, he stopped shaving—and said he wouldn't shave his beard until the company hit this goal. In June of 1998, Isuzu hit the number, and Bob shaved his beard in the company cafeteria in front of many employees. A brilliant symbolic celebration.

Other people we've known have brought in Starbucks coffee, or Krispy Kreme donuts, when small achievements were made. The point is to show that you understand that the battles—while minor, perhaps— were hard-fought. Symbolic celebrations encourage people to keep going and to reinforce that you know how hard Quadrant 2 can be.

As people get to the end of Quadrant 2, we hit another choice point: whether to go for gains or settle for performance that's just as good as when we started. This is a fairly easy decision to influence, since the "bummer zone" is now behind us.

One of our clients reorganized her department to facilitate better communication across "silos." The resulting J Curve was deep—Quadrants 1 and 2 lasted for three months. As the metrics she tracked slowly improved, she hit this decision point with her staff. At an all-hands meeting, she posed the question facing the team: "Do we keep reaping the benefits of what we've gone for, or do we settle for where we are?" One of her loud employees shouted out in a southern accent: "It's harvest time!" The group erupted in applause. The decision was made.

Quadrant 3 Coaching Tip: Big Goals

As Quadrant 3 begins, symbolic celebrations are no longer enough. At this point, the coach works with people to set goals so big they're scary. Jim Collins and Jerry Porras call these goals "BHAGs," short for "Big Hairy Audacious Goals."[2]

The pitfall in Quadrant 3 is setting goals too small to fully reap the benefits of having gone through the "bummer zone." A client John coaches was selling a business. In order to maximize its book value, his client had to change many things, including letting his staff work independently (so the business wouldn't be dependent on him) and letting go of key decisions. The resulting J Curve was tough. When he (and the business) emerged into Quadrant 3, he could set goals that were big enough to motivate him—in this case, the reward he'd receive for growing the business. He ended up selling the business for almost ten times its original book value before the J Curve.

The technique of setting big goals is fun. Ask your employees what they think is possible. In most cases, it'll be too small. One of our clients—using a technique we can't endorse, even though it works for him—yells at his employees (and his superiors) for being "narrow minded." "Think big!" he screams. For him, it works.

The key is to boost what people think is attainable. As the metric of success moves up, the top of Quadrant 3 gets extended—and so do the gains of the change process.

The Nexus Point

The final decision point is, for us, the only one that matters. People who decide not to start the change process drop off our radar—there's nothing we can do for them. People who opt out at the trough of the change probably wouldn't return our calls—to save face, they likely tell people the change didn't work. People who jump up and down as performance returns to historic levels will have gained a competence for change, but probably regard it largely as wasted time.

Our goal is to work exclusively with people and companies who have already gone through the J Curve on their own—as a result of corporate re-engineering, learning new skills, thinking about their values, or whatever else has driven them.

At the end of the J Curve is the real decision point for people who can become world class. As people maximize the gains from Quadrant 3, they can choose comfort—meaning they decide their changes have been enough, and they're done. The other choice is excellence—unlocking yet more potential, striving for even greater accomplishments.

If people choose excellence, they are choosing to repeat the change process, meaning another complete J Curve. The difference, though, is that a second J Curve's "bummer zone" is shallower and won't last as long. As people move through one J Curve after another, they build the competence to change, to learn, and to grow. Each J Curve ends with the choice—do we stop or do we keep going?

Tiger Woods was already world class in 1999 when he decided to further refine his stroke. He lost tournament after tournament as he moved through Quadrants 1 and 2. But as he progressed into Quadrant 3, people began to speculate that he might win all four major tournaments in one year (which he has since done). This level of performance is only possible for people who reach the nexus point of one change and decide to keep going.

Change As a Core Competence

As we establish a new millennium, futurists are quick to tell us what things will be like. One thing is certain—some will be right, most will be wrong. Our future prediction was simple, and we're certain we're right about it, because it's an assumption of every credible futurist we've ever read. Our prediction is that change will become faster, more profound, and more important. Those who learn to change will be leaders in businesses and leaders at the national and international levels. We suggest you make friends with the J Curve, because your future depends on it.

part four

Putting It All Together

A wise scholar once noted that when all you have is a hammer, everything looks like a nail. The "see," "say," "do" formula works. Yet there's a danger in treating it like a connect-the-dots process.

The purpose of this last section is to present coaching holistically. Each of the chapters takes the "see," "say," "do" concepts and applies them in some of the most common situations manager-coaches face. First, we'll look at how to integrate coaching with how managers report they spend the most time—solving problems. Second, we'll look at the learning reflex—a way of combining all the tools in this book and adapt them to your situation. Third, we'll look at situations when you might need to call in an expert (what we call "Coaching ER"). Finally, we'll look at coaching in situations when the four generations—Matures, the Baby Boomers, Generation X, and Generation Y—are all working together. Each of these chapters will help you to take the individual tools and weave them together into a coaching plan that will make you an outstanding manager-coach.

chapter twelve

The Art of Solving
the Right Problem

Ask a group of managers what their jobs entail, and it's almost certain that most will say something about decision making and problem solving. At many companies, the people who demonstrate high skill levels in these areas get promoted again and again, and end up in senior management. Or perhaps we should say, the people who convince others of their high skill levels in decision making and problem solving are the ones who get promoted.

Solving problems is a critical tool for the manager-coach—your employees will evaluate your success and your competence by how well you solve their problems. Your superiors will evaluate your potential for higher management by how well you solve their problems. More important, your customers will evaluate the success of your company by how well you solve their problems.

Two researchers, Landry[1] and Weick[2] looked carefully at the subject and elegantly defined the anatomy of a problem. So, let's define terms. For a problem to be a problem, four criteria must be obtained. First, there must be an event, whether past, present, or future, which is judged as negative. As we say in California, this is often a no-brainer. We worked with an entrepreneur who had run out of cash. As evidenced by the parentheses around his bank balance, his elevated blood pressure, and the beads of sweat that always seemed to cover his forehead, this was a negative event.

Second, there must be a "preliminary intention to intervene." Entrepreneur: "I gotta get cash."

Third, there must be an expression of the desire to allocate resources to solving the problem. Entrepreneur again: "I'd better spend some time raising cash, or I'm going to have a bigger problem."

Lastly, and importantly, there must be uncertainty as to the appropriate action to take. Entrepreneur again: "How am I going to raise the cash I need?"

We think that problem solving deserves special attention. The main reason is that decision-making starts with problems that we "see." Without a problem, there aren't many decisions to make. It's only when something is amiss that people must decide whether to change the course of their actions, and how to do so. If we identify the right problem to solve, often the right solution becomes obvious, and the decision is clear. Once people "say" what they'll do because of the problem, the rest usually follows.

The other main reason is that most people don't understand problem solving, and, as a result, aren't effective problem solvers. The key to problem solving, we believe, is identifying the *right* problem from the beginning and "saying" what you'll do about it.

The "Wrong Problem" Problem

Identifying the wrong problem has costs, some of which can be steep. For one, people try to solve the wrong problem over and over. Although this strategy is, at best, a low percentage solution—some might call it dumb—it seems to be popular. After all, they're invested in it now: it's been publicly identified as the problem. Solving it seems like an opportunity. Of course, while people are invested in solving the wrong problem, the right problem persists. Furthermore, solving the wrong problem can very well cause new problems, and then more time and effort is lost in applying wrong solutions to those. It can get very complicated. And time consuming. And expensive. Oh well, it's just (somebody else's) money, as they say.

Let's go back to our entrepreneur client. He had no cash, and he correctly identified that as a problem. It wasn't, though, the right problem. How does one solve the problem of "got no cash"? He gets cash. How does an entrepreneur get cash? The same way he's gotten cash before—from investors. So he spent two days on the phone with investors and he raised the money he needed to fund his operation for the next month.

What's the mistake here? Simple: he hasn't solved the right problem; he's only fed the cash monster for another month. In 30 days, he'll be in the same situation. Worse yet, the *real* problem—his business isn't profitable—has just gotten worse. He took time and money to increase his debt. He now needs to work extra hard to gain back his two days, and he's pushed his profitability off by probably another month, probably more because now the debt is larger. Ironically, the better he gets at solving the *wrong* problem, the worse the *real* problem will become.

In the coaching process, it's common for people to just disappear as clients. The usual reason is that the coaching has taken them out of their comfort zone. They are actually more comfortable operating as they have operated before. This entrepreneur is such a casualty—he just disappeared. Last we heard from him, he had taken a second and a third mortgage on his house, his company's debt was the highest it had ever been, and he was turning to his credit cards to fund his operation. He consistently refused to work on the *right* problem, so we weren't sorry to see him go. He never "saw" the right problem, so he couldn't make declarations consistent with success.

The Problem with Ivory Tower Problem Solvers

The reason for the few number of new, good books on this topic, we believe, is that down through time, people in universities and think tanks wrote the problem solving texts. Mostly the books just seem "out of touch" with solving real problems in the real world.

If you're a manager in a big company, you know about real problems—keeping a department together in a merger. If you manage a small company, you know a lot about more basic (and important) problems—keeping cash flow positive, making payroll.

We became very interested in this particular topic when Dave was asked to give a speech on "the art of solving the right problem." The timing was perfect, because our consulting company had hit a cash flow crunch—business was good, but companies were slow to pay us. We had to write out several large personal checks to make payroll. We had a problem.

So when we began reading book after book on the subject, we thought about the book's contents from the perspective of our problem. We read about decision tables, and evaluating the consequences of potential decisions. We read about rational decision-making, about defining the problem correctly. Then we turned to academic and professional articles on the topic. We slogged through thousands of pages, interviewed people who were considered experts on decision-making—including professors and business consultants.

As we investigated the topic more and more, we became increasingly frustrated. The ideas and tools made abstract sense. But it was a bit like being hungry and reading articles about how the body informs the brain that it is time to eat. We were hungry, and we were looking for food, not a dissertation on the digestive system.

A Little Myth, and How It Really Works

In the 1930s, a really bright guy named John Dewey wrote a book about problem solving. You've probably heard of Dewey before, as in the Dewey Decimal System. He wrote a book called *How We Think*,[3] and he wrote about a sequence of steps that you've probably heard of before: identify the problem, identify possible solutions, come up with criteria to evaluate the costs and benefits of potential solutions, and then choose the best solution. It's a good idea: it's logical, it's rational, and it makes good sense.

Most people, though, have misunderstood Dewey. He actually was proposing a way of thinking (in part), not just describing how thinking actually occurs. There is a big important difference between the two. Since the 1930s, we've come a long way in identifying psychological processes that underlie problem solving and decision-making.

Unfortunately, Dewey was off track (in part). Yet thousands of consultants and writers are traveling around the country, teaching people Dewey's system—with updated buzz phrases, of course.

We can illustrate how very simply. Think about what you had for breakfast this morning. Now ask the question: "Why did I eat that, and not something else?" Chances are, you now have a list of reasons, ranging from "it's healthy" to "I was really, really hungry."

At a speech on the art of solving the right problem that Dave delivered to a group of executives across Orange County in Southern California, he asked who had eaten the bacon at breakfast that morning, and why.

One person spoke for the group when he said: "It's free." (Actually, breakfast was included in the admission price.) Everyone laughed.

"But it was all free—so why did you choose the bacon over something else?"

"I don't get enough protein, and bacon has a lot of it."

"Why not the eggs, then? They also have a lot of protein."

"Well, I was really good yesterday—I went to the gym and I just thought I deserved it." Now most people were laughing.

When asked "why," he justified his behavior in a way that would bring a smile to Dewey—it sounded like he'd identified possible alternatives (no breakfast, eggs, bacon, etc.) and then evaluated each possibility against the criteria of "protein" and "enjoyability." In the end, he'd arrived at the only logical decision—bacon was the right choice, the best choice, for his problem. As laughter rippled through the audience, people began to "see" the absurdity of this man's position. He wanted bacon because he wanted bacon. So he chose to grab a lot of it.

It turns out, in actual fact, that's how most people make decisions.[4] They decide what to do at a gut level, and then they come up with reasons why that decision is best. This, by the way is a major *duh*. The two happen so fast that many people convince themselves that the reasons led to the decision, rather than the other way around. And that is a possible *aha*.

That's not to say people don't ever use reasons. For the most part, though, people get really invested in justifying decisions they've already made. Some of them get really good at it as well. After all, the people who become really good at justifying decisions seem more rational, more in control, more able to set the course for others—we call them managers. Oops.

Another persistent myth in problem solving holds that the person or people who identify a problem are the best ones to solve it. Again, this seems to make sense. You've probably seen some old war movie in which a young officer figures out a riddle that's driven everyone nuts, and an older general or admiral tells him to implement his solution. It's logical; it even seems fair. And usually, it's bad advice.

In decision-making, there are two divergent sets of skills, and it's rare that one person will have high competency in both skill sets. One skill set lies in problem identification. People who identify problems are usually creative, and often think in a non-linear way. This skill set requires one to be able to think beyond the "now," to envision numerous possible outcomes. Further, problem identifiers rely on the input of others, but aren't necessarily swayed by any given opinion. They're able to sift through many points of view.

Solution implementers have a different skill set altogether, and different competencies. These people think in a more linear way. They're task-oriented and often more effective at managing the politics of getting things done. Selling others on the chosen solution is an important part of this skill set. Solution implementers have the ability to focus on the details while at the same time keeping their eye on the big picture.

Again, we try to practice what we preach. John is better at identifying problems while Dave is better at implementing solutions. Both of us are really good at justifying our reasons. We've learned—the hard way—that we should let each person do what he's good at doing.

What about you? Are you more linear or do your best ideas come from "intuitive leaps"? Problem identifiers are often people who are easily distracted, with the ability to apply lessons from one field to another. Albert Einstein was such a person. So is Disney's Michael Eisner.

DayTimers and PalmPilots are the tools that usually drive solution implementers. These folks are highly structured, even a little "anal." They think in details and constantly ask themselves the question: "Have I left anything undone?" The other ones, the problem identifiers, like to look at the big picture and usually couldn't care less about the details. They think that all that detail stuff tends to work itself out. John really enjoys watching Dave working with his PalmPilot.

It's good to know which role you use naturally. It's also good advice to make sure your team includes people who can do both.

The importance of this difference is highlighted in the story of Daniel, the general manager in a large division of an Australian telecommunications company. An initial assessment showed that he was achievement-focused and highly introverted, typical of people who are good solution implementers. Daniel used the Personal Learning Index[5] to "see" that he learned best by doing—he's an "action learner." Daniel also came to "see" that only about a third of people learn best this way—a third are "people learners" (learning by interacting with people), and a third are "information learners" (learning from data).

Putting all this together, Daniel "saw" that he needed to quickly develop his influencing skills so he could more effectively head up his major business unit.

Together with his coach, Amy Powell of Development Partners, Daniel worked on developing an approach to consultation (the "say" step). He drew up a list of all the people who needed to be "on his side" for this new initiative to be successful. He worked on his listening skills, and developed a way to approach and engage each person (the "do" step). He learned the value of listening to these people first, rather than trying to bulldoze his ideas through. While this new way of doing things felt rather awkward at first, he persevered. And he got results.

At the end of his coaching, Daniel had achieved a successful start-up for the new business initiative, and subsequently headed up a major cost-saving initiative that saved his division millions of dollars. His boss, the CEO, stated that Daniel "never would have gotten the project through" without the highly consultative approach he took. Several months after his coaching was complete, Daniel reported:

"One of the most significant things is that consultation has become second nature to me . . . it's just something I find myself doing unconsciously. I often find myself explaining the importance of consultation to my own managers, and teaching them how to do it."

By "seeing" that he was a solution implementer, and that he needed to work with people who were more problem identifiers, Daniel recognized the new skills he had to learn. His coach worked with him until he "said" what actions he would take to make a bigger impact in his job.

Snapping Ideas Together

Leonardo Da Vinci solved a lot of problems in his day. From the design of helicopters to contact lenses, his track record is among the best of all time.

Da Vinci used a system of thinking that went back to the ancient Greeks. The Greeks took for granted that every so often, the gods would reach down and zap them with a little bit of inspiration. Pythagoras, for example, had a flash of inspiration about the relationships of the sides of a triangle. And then, like other Greeks, Pythagoras strolled down to a public meeting place and began talking to other people. Some of them probably knew something about mathematics, but others certainly didn't. What Pythagoras and his friends (the people who invented things like medicine and democracy and logic) knew is that they didn't have the whole, finished idea. The gods had given them a piece of it, and to do something worthwhile with that bit of inspired thought, they would have to work in concert with others to expand it.

Da Vinci used this principle. He expected these sparks of inspiration to hit. And he spent a great deal of time talking to people, some of whom knew nothing about mathematics, or art, or anatomy, because he knew that the sparks of inspiration only gave him partial ideas—which needed time and input to develop into something more useful.

Talking with people whose background is different from yours about your problems is a vital and valuable skill for manager-coaches to develop. When we start taking for granted that every so often we (and the people around us) will have a little inspiration, and that inspiration will be a starting point for more discussion, we become open not just to the inspiration itself, but also to the input of others. Other people and other points of view are not a threat, but allies and arguments that will aid and shape a better idea. Great coaches are always looking and listening for the coaching of others.

We worked with an entrepreneur who had a small software company, and no one was buying his products. It was easy for him to identify all kinds of problems, or so he thought. After all, a big one was staring him in the face: nobody wanted to buy what he was selling. And then one night on an airplane, the spark hit. "Aha," he said, "I don't want to be in the software business, I want to be in the relationship business. I want a small, select group of clients, instead of trying to sell my products to everyone I can." In this moment of inspiration, the

entrepreneur had come closer to solving his problem simply by identifying the right problem: he wasn't in the right business. It's easy to see
that this inspiration didn't give him the whole problem, or certainly a
whole solution. There was still plenty of work to do. But he had taken
a critically important first step toward getting out of the whirlpool he'd
been in.

The "do" for manager-coaches is simple: encourage an atmosphere
of free thinking, free discussion, and brainstorming. Ask each person to
freely discuss his or her professional problems with colleagues. In an
analysis of what makes some groups work while others don't, Warren
Bennis and Patricia Ward Biederman found that brainstorming and
open sharing of ideas is one of the hallmarks of truly great teams.[6] If
you encourage this behavior in your team, you'll be tapping the same
creative genius that Da Vinci, Edison, and the Greeks used to solve
their problems.

The Simplistic Solution Paradox

One of the most vexing aspects of problem solving for many business-
people is that they fall easily into what we call the "simplistic solution
paradox." This is a definite don't. The "got no cash" entrepreneur we
discussed earlier had fallen into this pit—the problem he was trying to
solve was much more basic than his *real* problem of not having a profitable business. Sadly, trying to solve the simplistic problem makes the
real problem worse, as we saw in his case.

Here's an example of how another entrepreneur stepped over the
"simplistic solution paradox" and fixed the real problem. We worked
with an inventor who had patented a chemical product. He had the
same problem—a constant negative cash flow, since his first product
would take years to get through testing, certification, and into the
market.

When we began to work with him, we first had him "see" that he
was looking at the wrong problem—negative monthly cash flow—and it

would only make things worse if he focused just on that. Once he "saw" the real problem—no means of creating long-term cash flow for years—potential solutions began popping in his mind. One of these solutions was to hold an auction to license his first patented chemical product. In the end, he received less from this product by selling the rights before it was fully tested, but he solved the real problem—his business got both a large infusion of cash and a handsome monthly royalty. This gave him the flexibility to work on several other chemical products, which he now had the cash to take to market himself. By sidestepping the "simplistic solution," he started running a profitable business.

Some people respond, "The simplistic solution paradox wouldn't happen to me, because I think outside the box!" This is dangerous and flawed thinking based on a misreading or, more likely, a sloppy misinterpretation of one of the most important books of the last century—*The Structure of Scientific Revolutions.*[7] In the book, Thomas Kuhn argues that science doesn't really jump from discovery to discovery the way we're taught in high school. Rather, people in the old "box" die and then that box is replaced with a new way of thinking. Galileo's discovery of stars and planets had to wait for the religiously dogmatic zealots of his day to die before his ideas could enter the mainstream of science. Kuhn called the "box" of an age its "paradigm." Sadly, when popular culture grabbed hold of his thinking, we started telling each other to "shift our paradigms" (impossible, in 99 percent of cases) and to "get out of the box." According to Kuhn, the only way out of the box is to die. And then, they put us in another box (probably pine), and we stay in this one for a very long time.

When you coach your employees in problem solving, you'll see that several are, sadly, stuck in the simplistic solution paradox. Unfortunately, saying "Hey, you're in a simplistic solution trap" doesn't do much good.

The way out of this trap is to use the "go deep" listening technique to help employees realize for themselves that their solution will cause other bigger problems. You might hear a *duh* as they realize their mistake. When they "see" the problem for themselves, you will be able to coach them on better approaches to problem solving.

The "Red Herring"

Another easy trap to get snared in is the "red herring." This is another don't. In this trap, someone attempts to solve a problem before they know what the heck is going on. We know this is hard to believe, but people actually do that. There's a well-known story of an Indian government official who spotted what seemed to be the signs of plague in his city. In a state of alarm, he went on radio and television to warn people. Tens of thousands attempted to flee the city in a state of panic and hundreds of people died needlessly in tramplings and accidents. The wave of illness turned out not to be plague after all. It was a "red herring."[8]

While we doubt that company problems would include outbreaks of rodent-borne illness, the example is useful because it shows the importance of understanding as much of the scope and scale of a given problem as one can, before one acts. Here again, it's extremely useful to talk to people, to accumulate many divergent points of view, and to see what sparks of inspiration (if any) might hit.

Of course, another common scenario when an organization faces a problem is that people don't think about the problem at all. Either they've already rushed into solving what they think the problem might be (in other words, they're busily solving the wrong problem) or they've become ostriches, burying their heads in the sand and hoping that the difficulty passes on its own. Perhaps they work in a department where action and results are valued above everything else. Sitting quietly and thinking about a problem might not look like time well spent in a place like that, but there's a danger: what if no one is thinking at all? This is where—and when—those flashes of inspiration just might hit. Thinking about problems is time well spent. Think about it.

It's inevitable that from time to time, we'll make the wrong decisions. Regardless of our stature in business, we're still human, and fallible. But too often, people will spend valuable executive time justifying poor decisions, rather than making a better decision through better problem solving.

Focus on Future Accomplishments, Not the Immediate Problem

The trick here is simple—project the course of the present situation five or six years into the future. From that perspective, look back at today. Then ask the question: "What problem should I have been working on back then?" This will get you focused on accomplishments, rather than on simplistic solutions that might create other problems.

Remember the chemical-products inventor? When he identified what he wanted to accomplish (a profitable company capable of sustaining itself), it was much easier for him to begin seeing solutions separate from spending all his time raising capital. In other words, he saw beyond the problem in front of him by thinking out several years.

The Walking-Talking White Paper

We've discussed how the Greeks, and Da Vinci, would wander down to a gathering place and talk about the inspirations they'd been having. That's not always directly possible in today's workplace, but here's a great tool to take advantage of the same principle. We call it "the walking-talking white paper."[9]

The manager-coach sees what she thinks is a problem, and writes up everything she knows about it. She sends this "white paper" around with a call for input. Sure, she might get a few strange e-mails and perhaps even a cocked eyebrow or two, but soon, something brilliant begins to happen. The "white paper" comes back with lots of sticky-notes all over it, writing in the margins, stuff crossed out, new pages put in, and so forth. The manager-coach returns to her office and rewrites the white paper, sending it around again with notes about the inclusion of everyone's input.

And then something *really* brilliant begins to happen. Other people see their input coming to bear on the white paper. They get invested in the problem and its possible solutions. Soon lots of people have something to "say," and they're actively involved in identifying the problem and in implementing solutions. This is the goal of the "walking-talking white paper" tool.

Management consultant Beverly Kaye uses this tool to launch new development efforts in *Fortune* 500 companies. She "stealth" coaches (provides coaching that isn't seen by most people in the company) a manager in the corporation to write up his idea in a "walking-talking white paper" and to send it around. Then, before the rewrite, she coaches him on how to include people's input. By combining expert coaching with the ego boost people get from seeing their ideas added to the "walking-talking white paper," the approach easily and effectively solves many tough corporate problems.

A Few More Problem-Solving Tools

- **Go for the Brilliantly Simple Solution.** Rather than focusing on simplistic solutions, look for the simple solution that is brilliant in its ability to solve the problem without creating new problems. Again, recall our chemical-products inventor. When he saw what he wanted to accomplish, it wasn't long before a simple, but brilliant, solution emerged—auction the license to use his patented product. It's a brilliantly simple solution because it solves his immediate problem and lets him focus on what he's good at doing—inventing chemical stuff.

- **"What would _____ do here?"** Start thinking about someone you greatly admire, possibly from a completely different field. This might even be a hero to you—Abraham Lincoln, Rosa Parks, or Jack Welch. Next time you're stopped by a problem, ask yourself what he or she would do. This may not lead immediately to the solution itself, but it might lead to that spark of inspiration, or get you thinking in a new way. One manager we worked with would often ask himself: "What would Captain Kirk do here?"

Amazingly, this worked for him—and helped him spot the *real* problem several times.

- **Know *everything* about the problem AND know *nothing* about the problem.** As we saw from Da Vinci, it's a great idea to talk to people who don't have the background you have, while at the same time using all your training and education to solve a problem. Ultimately, this is the only way to get "out of the box"—by talking to people who are in different "boxes," people who know virtually nothing about the problem. Einstein considered some of the most insightful people in his life poets and philosophers, because they encouraged him to think in completely new directions.

- **Ride the "zero-gravity plane."** We worked with a defense contractor who was trying to re-engineer an entire division. The entire senior management got together and wrote down all the steps it took to get a contract, design and build a product, and get paid—over 300 steps. In a session that ran until 2 A.M., the team reduced that to a mere 13 steps. The next morning, the managers were tired but jazzed. One of them shared the brilliant 13 steps with one of the people at the "bottom" of the organization (according to the chart hanging on the wall). He listened, and responded, in total deadpan, "That's great—except it requires me to solder parts that I don't get for another two steps." *Duh.* If you've seen the movie *Apollo 13*, you might remember the scenes when Tom Hanks and the other astronauts seemed to float. The actors actually were floating, in a specially designed plane that would climb to high altitudes, and then plummet. During the steep descents, gravity dropped to almost nothing, and the actors could float around like real astronauts. The metaphor here is that solutions and problems need to be examined at both very high altitudes—what the senior management team did—and from the "rank-and-file" perspective before we can put any faith in them. The "to-do" in the "zero gravity plane" is to test your ideas at all levels, and be open to criticism, before trying to implement an idea that might put you out of business.

The Witches' Brew

There's a popular and effective problem solving technique identified by several academics as "the garbage can method."[10] In this technique, throw together all of this: problems, solutions, people, and some choice opportunities, and stir. "Stir" means letting time pass, and letting people talk. Most problems will clarify themselves and solutions will float to the top very quickly. We'll end with this tool because it ties together many of the themes from this chapter.

We refer to this method as "The Witches' Brew" because frankly, it sounds better than "garbage can," and because we're always looking for a way to quote Shakespeare:

> Fillet of a fenny snake,
> In the cauldron boil and bake;
> Eye of newt, and toe of frog,
> Wool of bat, and tongue of dog;
> Adder's fork, and blind-worm's sting,
> Lizard's leg, and howlet's wing;
> For a charm of powerful trouble,
> Like a hell-broth boil and bubble.
> Double, double, toil and trouble;
> Fire burn and cauldron bubble.
> —*Macbeth*, Act IV, Scene I

Here are some of the things we like about this method of problem solving. We'll follow this up with some tools for how to stir up a pot of Witches' Brew for your team.

Problem solving takes time, and it's rarely easy. There's a persistent myth, perhaps especially in the United States, glamorizing lone decision makers quietly churning out one tough decision after the next. It's easy to get wrapped up in that model and to think that we should be strong, silent, and gutsy, making those tough decisions all alone and forcing the people we work with to go along with them.

Research shows clearly that groups make better decisions than individuals, however. This information tends to tick off people who operate at the "useful" level, but those managing at "important" and "vital" immediately recognize the truth in it. This group method is better because other people are invested in the decision and solving the problem. After all, since they helped create the solution, people tend to implement and follow through more effectively. The well-known children's story of "Stone Soup" provides an example.

Recall that at the beginning of the story, a young boy asked a man what he was eating. "Stone soup," replied the man, who soon suggested that the soup, while great, would be better with some carrots. Carrots were fetched, others gathered, and it wasn't long before the entire town began to participate in the magic of making stone soup. Potatoes found their way in, and meat. Other vegetables arrived too, and soon the soup expanded, got better, and fed the entire town. At the end of the story the man who started the soup with the stone turned to the young boy and told him that he could use the magic stone to make stone soup any time. All he had to do was start with that rock, and go from there, just as they had together on that day.

In addition to being a favorite children's story, it's a powerful example of how groups of people can perform better—they can make a fuller, richer soup—than individuals working alone.

How does a manager-coach put together a Witches' Brew session? All it takes is people, a place, some time, and the willingness to follow a few rules.

Take people from lots of different disciplines, if possible, or at the very least, take people with differing points of view, and differing approaches not just to the problem at hand, but to problem solving itself ("eye of newt, and toe of frog, wool of bat and tongue of dog"). Put them into the "cauldron" to "boil and bake." In other words, sit down together and start talking.

Brainstorming rules apply in Witches' Brew sessions: there aren't any right or wrong answers and *nothing* is stupid. Add some input if things begin to go off track. Stick to the problem at hand—or what the problem seems to be—while allowing for new approaches to emerge. The conversation might bubble and become frothy, but keep the heat high and let possible solutions bubble up to the surface. Stir them around among the group; they'll sink back down, and bubble back up in a different way. Eventually, new insights, new approaches, and new points of view will emerge, and that's where the magic happens.

Louis Koster, the physician-turned consultant we met in an earlier chapter, recently organized a meeting of several warring groups in the Middle East. "I helped both sides to 'see' the situation differently, and that they had some control over the situation. When they 'said' what they intended to do, amazing things happened."

Of course, in running a Witches' Brew session, there are some things to guard against. Often in organizations, powerful people dominate simply because they are forceful. There is a big difference between being a powerful person and being a forceful person in a position of power. Others may defer to them, unwilling to challenge them due to fear of reprisal. It should be clear that this won't work in a Witches' Brew session: it leads to "group-think," in which the entire group goes along with a dominant member or two. Manager-coaches avoid this by ensuring that Witches' Brew sessions are kept confidential, and also by setting clear guidelines for the discussion. If group-think begins to emerge, the facilitator (the manager-coach) must intervene to stir the cauldron again.

The benefit of these sessions should be clear: something unexpected will emerge as the discussion stirs, boils, and bubbles. The solution to the problem will be richer, better, more effective than it would have been had any single person attempted to create it. And when people leave a session like this, they're invested in solving the problem, because after all, they helped to invent the solution. People feel valued, and they act accordingly.

The Apollo missions were great examples of the Witches' Brew concept in action. At that time, NASA brought together engineers, psychologists, researchers in chemistry, ergonomics, geology, engineering, computer science, and people from numerous other disciplines, and together they solved a myriad of problems en route to putting a man on the moon. They were able to do so because everyone shared the same overall vision, and everyone participated in creating solutions to the challenges the program faced.

The biggest objection we hear to this suggestion is that it takes time, and managers' time is very valuable. We agree. A "Witches' Brew" can take hours to cook up, or it can happen in the time it takes to make a pot of coffee. The time spent is a function of the ground rules. Most "Witches' Brews" take months, but they can happen in brief moments as people naturally interact. But they won't happen at all if manager-coaches don't see value in people talking about their off-the-wall ideas.

In summary, problem solving is tough, and most people mess it up. The truth about problem solving is that most people fool themselves into thinking that they've carefully thought through an issue, when they're really going with their gut instinct. The solution is to use techniques like those in this chapter that jolt us into new ways of thinking about the issue. The key is to remember that the best solutions come to us when we talk with people who have different perspectives and backgrounds. Like Da Vinci and the Greeks, we just might connect our inspiration with others, and produce a solution to a problem that changes the world.

chapter thirteen

The Effectiveness

Reflex

At the end of the twentieth century, disasters were big business. The movie *Titanic* set box office records and spawned a documentary from just about every cable network. Movies about viral outbreaks, nuclear war, terrorist plots, and Y2K filled both network time and movie theaters.

Planning for disasters is now a bigger part of design budgets than ever before. Webmasters have to plan for catastrophic crashes and building engineers have to anticipate 8.5 earthquakes in areas previously thought to be quake-free. The field that arguably includes the most disaster planning is the design of submarines.

Since first introduced, about 39 American subs have been lost, sometimes causing the deaths of everyone on board.[1] As a result, today's subs are designed with just about every contingency in mind.

One of the first lessons for sub designers was the importance of airtight compartments. People on board the *Titanic* thought the boat had airtight compartments, but all it really had were walls that rose about eight decks.[2] When water flooded more than two of the compartments, the boat tilted and water gushed over the walls from one compartment to the next, sinking the "unsinkable."

As a result of this lesson, today's subs have, as a first line of defense against hull breaches, many airtight compartments that can be completely closed. One can flood without affecting the next, unlike the *Titanic.* This design has been credited with saving several submarines when the worst-case scenarios came true. The metaphor of the submarine with airtight compartments is useful for manager-coaches to ensure that their employees learn from their experiences and act effectively in as many situations as possible.

Processing Processes

For decades, psychologists have researched and popularized the idea that people move through stages when their circumstances change. One of the most famous of these processes is the "grief cycle," in which people move from shock and denial to anger to bargaining to depression and finally to acceptance.[3] People move through these stages naturally, say many psychologists, and may move forward, then back, and forward again. It's a bit like sea water sloshing through the compartments of boats whose compartments weren't airtight.

People also move through different stages when they learn from experience. One of the giants in this line of research is Kolb, who wrote that people must move through four stages of thought to truly learn and apply lessons learned through experience.[4] Unlike the grief cycle, Kolb argues that people need to be led through his four stages and that the stages should be distinct from each other.

We combined the work of Kolb and other psychologists, along with some of the best research in coaching, to produce what we call the "effectiveness reflex." This is a series of four stages that manager-coaches lead employees through to ensure that they don't repeat the same mistake over and over. We go further than Kolb's advice—we argue that this cycle only works if the stages are like the airtight compartments of a modern submarine. Before a person moves from the first stage to the second, he has to "finish his business," move into the next compartment, and seal the door. Once a door is sealed, the previous compartment is flooded, and the person can't return. When a stage is passed through and completed, it is done.

This metaphor is based on coaching horror stories. You've probably heard something similar to one of these horror stories if you ever listen to call-in psychology shows on talk radio. The second-worst pattern is when the caller says what the problem is, the psychologist responds with her advice, and then just seconds before she has to break for a commercial, his voice trails in with, "Oh, that won't work. I forgot to tell you something." It seems like wasted time for everyone—the caller, the psychologist, and thousands or millions of people listening.

The worst pattern in call-in shows happens when the psychologist offers advice when she doesn't have all the facts and doesn't know it. If the person takes the advice, his situation may worsen because the advice is flawed. Coaching is not psychology, strictly speaking, and the mechanism that underlies it is different. Yet if people don't get out all the facts before moving on, the rest of the "effectiveness reflex" won't work, since all the information won't be in the mix.

Stage One: What Happened?

Stage One of the effectiveness reflex begins when the employee tells you what happened in a situation. It can be a success or a failure, or a mixed situation. But the employee has to be honest and forthcoming about everything that happened.

Many employees will be eager to share their successes, but will keep their failures to themselves. Actually, it's especially important to "process" failures, since you—as the manager-coach—are responsible for the employee's learning and growth. Employees who repeat the same mistakes over and over are probably in a spin—and they won't do their jobs effectively. Some might even criticize you for not doing yours.

We worked with a manager who had a habit of making people angry. It was a consistent pattern in his life, going far beyond his job duties. He routinely irritated his friends, alienated his wife, and ticked off his neighbors. We worked with him for a year to break this "spin." Like most people, he "ate" these failures and didn't want to talk about them. This normally gregarious person would get very quiet and barely speak. One day, though, he crossed the line with a superior in a failure that became public. He couldn't "eat" this one.

When first meeting with him, we asked him what happened. "Oh, I said the wrong thing." In this first stage, we're only looking for a review of the events. No interpretations, no labeling, no justifications. He gave us an analysis of what happened, not the facts.

"That's an analysis. Tell us what happened." He started off the story saying why it wasn't a big deal. Again, we had to stop him.

"You're jumping ahead. If you don't go through these stages in order and completely, you won't learn as much as you can from this situation, and you'll repeat the mistake in the future." Finally, he told us the facts from start to finish—the whole story. He had been in a series of meetings to implement a new operating procedure in his company, and he got angry at someone he thought was a peer—but who had much more power and authority than he had—and this person was now publicly embarrassing our manager friend in e-mails to people across the company.

"Is there anything else, anything you haven't told us that happened?" we asked.

"No, that's it."

"Are you sure? We're about to seal this compartment and move on. Once we do, you won't be able to go back. Is there anything else?"

He then told us the core detail in the story—he had told one of his subordinates exactly what he thought of this other person, and his subordinate had told the superior. Not only was his superior angry about the events of the meeting, he was deeply offended by the graphic nature of the label the manager had used to describe him. This is not good.

When you use the effectiveness reflex with your employees, you'll notice people's strong tendency to conceal the more embarrassing—and most important—piece of information until you're about ready to flood the compartment. When they know it's their last opportunity to add facts, they'll often tell the truth—the whole truth.

Many managers who have been trained in active listening will move from this stage to giving advice. Don't do it. The effective manager-coach relies on the employee's good sense and intelligence to solve his own problems. But before we can get to solutions, we first have to let the employee vent.

Stage Two: Why It's Not Your Fault

At the end of Stage One, most employees will be thinking: "This really isn't my fault." Or at least, "It's not completely my fault." We need to process this objection before moving on.

In Stage Two, you invite the person to give you all the reasons why he's a victim, isn't responsible for what happens, is the target of a conspiracy, or whatever else comes up. We started Stage Two by saying: "You mentioned you think this isn't all your fault. Say more about that."

Then it all came out—this superior was stupid, and saw this manager as a threat. He has a reputation for "taking people out," isn't fair, and probably "everyone knows" his marriage is in trouble because he's such a jerk all the time.

Then more came out. This manager was just doing his job, he was betrayed by his subordinate; "we all know" the company won't defend me; HR will take his side, and so on.

And then the snowstorm became a blizzard. "This company sucks," he said, rising from his chair. "It just promotes people who brown-nose. They don't care about people like me who get things done. I've done more than him, and everyone knows that. Yet, I bet he makes double what I do."

After nearly a half an hour, the blizzard ripped through the office. "Anything else?" we asked.

"No," he said. He seemed apologetic that he had said some of the things he did. We reminded him of the safe environment we all agreed to. We told him that we were about to leave the second compartment, and it would be flooded with icy seawater. No return.

"I'm ready," he said.

Notice that this second stage is necessary even when employees are reporting a victory, rather than a train wreck. In many cases, their victory story will include a theme that they overcame the odds—"the bastards didn't get me down," as Patton might have said.

Without this second stage, the lesson they will remember is that they can overcome the odds. They'll remember a competitive struggle in which their brains and natural abilities, along with hard work, won the day. Outside Hollywood, most incidents aren't this simple. The goal of the "effectiveness reflex" is to help people learn all the lessons they can, and integrate these lessons into their future behavior.

Stage Three: What Could You Have Done Differently?

In Stage Three, you reverse course. Instead of asking how the person was a victim, you assume that he is 100 percent responsible for the events. Given the circumstances, how could this person have acted more wisely?

"I probably couldn't," the manager responded to our question. "I was doomed from the start and didn't know it."

"You just went back to Stage Two, and we're not doing that," we reminded him.

Grudgingly, the manager spat out: "I suppose I shouldn't call people names."

"What else?"

"I shouldn't have told [my subordinate] what I thought."

"What else?"

He became angry. "I don't know. I should have been smarter, better, taller, and I should have gone to Harvard," he yelled.

We had to remind him that he had just reverted to Stage Two again, and we weren't going to listen to him if he stayed there. After all, he was the one who said that he was ready to move on.

"That's all I can think of."

Here's the test of whether Stage Three is really done: "Okay, if you didn't call him names and didn't spill your gripes to your employee, would this whole situation have been prevented?"

"Yes," he said, looking down.

"Really?"

"No. I suppose I have a way of making enemies."

"What could you have done differently?"

"I suppose I should have given him regular updates on my progress, rather than fighting him. I should have tried to partner with him."

"Good. Would this behavior have prevented this situation?"

"Yes," he said, this time looking us in the eye.

"Are we ready to move on? Same rules—we're going to flood Stage Three and you can't come back here."

"Yes," he declared.

Stage Four: What Will You Commit to Doing Differently in the Future?

"I'll try to form effective partnerships with people I don't naturally get along with," he said.

"And how will you do this?"

"I'll identify people I don't like and try to bring them on the team." Notice that he just declared—the "say" step—that he would elevate himself beyond the "important culture" by getting rid of the "us-them" separation.

"Like who?"

He listed off three people.

"What will you do with each of them?"

He reported his plan for each person, including an initial step of going to lunch with each one individually.

"When will you have this initial step done?" we asked.

"I'll call today." He has now completed the "say" step.

"Great," John said. "I'll call you tomorrow to follow up." Notice that the client completed a "contract" with the coach, and since this person hasn't earned complete trust yet, he belongs in the "high management, low trust" box. We set up an interim check to make sure he follows through.

We kept him on Stage Four until he declared what he would do with his employee (have an open discussion with him, in which he would apologize for putting his subordinate in a difficult position), what he would do with this superior he had irritated (meet with him and "bury the hatchet" in a private meeting), and how he would stop the gripe cycle sweeping through his department (have an all-hands meeting in which he would admit his mistake, apologize for not living up to his own standards, and declare he would act differently in the future). We set up follow-up checks with him to make sure he performed each action he committed to taking.

Finally, we were ready to end the discussion. "We're done. Is there anything else you want to say?" we asked.

"No, I'm ready to make these phone calls." We left, and he picked up the phone. He was up to the "do" stage of the coaching cycle.

It took several months, but he restored his reputation. He later left that job. Armed with a great letter from his boss, he took another job with a significant increase in pay. More importantly, to the best of our knowledge, he never repeated the mistake of picking a fight again.

Coaching in a Box

The value of the four stages of the effectiveness reflex is that they summarize everything in this book in one method. If you create a safe environment, the person will usually open up and talk about their failures, and their successes. They'll also "see" where they could have been more effective, they'll "say" what they'll do differently, and the coach can help take them through the "do" step by managing "contracts" between the coach and the client.

Notice that this method also elevates people up through the cultures, all the way to the vital level, by asking them how they can do things better in the future. It automatically converts their gripes into requests, and eventually into "contracts." If the employee hasn't earned your trust, you can make sure they follow through by using the "high management, low trust" management box. But once the employee has proven he can take these steps on his own, shift to the "high trust, low management" box.

Yet there are some employees who won't respond to this method. If people are dedicated to remaining victims, or maintaining the "life sucks" theme, you'll find the airtight door between Stages Two and Three won't close.

Our advice when this happens is to abort the process and stop. Some people, for whatever reason, are not coachable. Rather than giving yourself a migraine and the employee a reason to complain about you, we have two mottos to keep in mind:

1. Don't wrestle with pigs. You only get dirty and the pig likes it.
2. Work with the living. Don't try to raise the dead.

Sadly, people firmly embedded in the "undermining" and "ineffective" cultures are totally convinced that there's absolutely nothing they can do. Not only that, but they've gathered evidence and the agreement of the people around them to support their point of view. These people are usually bulletproof when it comes to coaching. Like guests on daytime talk shows, they feel liberated, enlightened, and "right" about this belief. They'll even enjoy teaching a foolish person like you why they're "right" and you're "wrong." They'll relate stories about when they thought optimistically and naïvely like you, and how they learned. They might even suck you into their sad story.

When you introduce coaching into your management style, some people will take to it and others won't. We suggest you get coaching on your coaching to learn how to sharpen your own skills. But remember that if people don't take to your methods, they probably aren't future world-class championship team level employees. It's good to know this now, rather than waste your (and their) time.

Why a Reflex?

Some people ask why we call this four-stage process a "reflex," rather than a method. The reason is that for it to work, you have to use it reliably, almost religiously, until it's something that happens automatically, like the Patella Reflex. Once in place, this reflex will help you to live an "examined life"; you'll be "de-spinning yourself" all the time, to reference Socrates, Emerson, and your two humble authors.

Emerson kept a journal throughout his life, beginning when he attended Harvard. He used this journal to not only record his thoughts, but to evaluate his actions. While Emerson wasn't so formulaic as to use something like our four-step process, it did help him learn lessons and not repeat mistakes.

Every year, Dave reviews his journal in late December. It usually numbers more than 200 pages, and records his successes and failures. Most important, it also records his dedications for improvement. "I'm far from perfect about implementing each one, but having done this for more than a decade, I can look back and see that I haven't lived the same year twice. I've repeated mistakes, but I haven't repeated most more than twice," Dave said.

"Late in December, I write a long entry in my journal using these four steps on the entire year. What happened? How was I a victim of circumstances? What could I have done differently? What will I commit to doing differently in the future?"

The themes from the last step become a declaration that I live throughout the next year. I intend to practice what I preach, I tell my friends and family about my declaration, and ask for their help, insights, and coaching. It is through this process, and the help from my friends, that I completed two masters degrees and a doctorate, found a professorship when the economy was eliminating these positions (especially at research universities), and started a (now) successful consulting company.

We offer this combination—a journal and the effectiveness reflex— as a way to make sure you always learn, rarely spin, and become a manager-coach. We hope you find it useful.

chapter fourteen

Coaching ER

At the end of every fiscal year, the employees of our consulting company gather around a large restaurant table to celebrate the past 12 months. We usually retell a lot of stories about the great things that happened, and about the not-so-great things that happened. After a few drinks, one of us will toast to "the client most deserving to have a novel written about them." Last year, the winner of this toast was a nonprofit organization that hired us to straighten out their board. Our efforts would have worked—if the president weren't having an affair with the treasurer, who was secretly embezzling money to pay for his divorce from the chairman's secretary. These naughty children were going nuts, keeping their respective acts together while trying to pull off this rather imaginative caprice. It was like a bad soap opera. A simultaneous violation of all three of JLS's Core Values—not ethical, no fun, and the nonprofit was dripping in red ink. And to top it off, they acted surprised and upset when we busted them and walked. Imagine that. As the great jazz musician Charlie Byrd once said, "There's nothing more far out than people."

Most of our stories, though, are about how amazing our clients are. Yet even the amazing ones can get themselves in trouble by not knowing when the manager-coach should call for help.

Many of our clients work in health care—from physicians who own practices to executives in biotechnology. People in health care are usually big believers in everyone knowing CPR. The danger, one our ER physician-friends recently explained, is that knowing CPR makes people feel like they know more than they do. "The most important part of first aid," he said, "is knowing how to dial 911."

The purpose of this chapter is to lay out the boundaries of good coaching. If you stay within these lines, you'll almost always be an effective manager-coach. When you find yourself outside a boundary, it's time to follow our friend's advice and dial 911.

Sources of Help

There are many sources of help for manager-coaches. One of the most effective is the corporate HR department of most big companies. Most HR generalists, and professionals in training and development, are eager to work with managers who "get" coaching.

The best source of help is often an outside coach. We recently interviewed Marian Baker, a senior coach in Chicago, who talks about how manager-coaches can find coaches for themselves. "Talk to three or four good, experienced coaches until you find someone you click with," she said. "Bring an issue or problem to them and see how helpful they are. Each session will be valuable—it will help you with whatever your issues are."

Your HR department probably knows of some good coaches. You can also visit our Web site for links to coaching organizations and profiles on some of America's best coaches. We're at *www. coachingrevolution.com.*

Several Hats, One Head

Managers have several jobs they have to perform at once. Objective setter. Evaluator. Resource planner. These roles sometimes require them to enforce standards, such as minimum requirements. This, Marian Baker explained, can make the job of manager-coach confusing to subordinates:

"A coach elicits people's hopes and wants, and facilitates them moving in that direction. A coach is just there for the client, while a manager is there for both the employee and for the company. Whenever this seems strange or in conflict, a manager-as-coach should step away from the coaching role and bring in a truly neutral person."

Other coaches we interviewed agree. A manager-coach must protect the safe coaching environment or the coaching process will collapse. When an employee is on probation, under suspicion for anything, or is in danger of disciplinary action, a manager-coach has to make a tough call: is it better to coach this person or act purely as his or her manager?

Most of the experts we interviewed believe the choice should lie with the employee, but that the choice must *really* be a choice. We talked with a senior manager in a large manufacturing company who crossed this line without knowing the line even existed.

"I had a subordinate, a manager who reported to me, who just wasn't hitting his metrics," she said. "I explained how I could coach him, and then asked what he'd prefer. 'You,' he said, as if the decision was obvious. I felt validated—like I was the best manager-coach ever.

"The next week, I talked with him about what he really wanted. We were chatting and then, all of a sudden, he just stopped talking. I asked him what was going on and he just shrugged. After five awkward minutes, we ended the session.

"About an hour later, I asked him if he wanted to get a cup of coffee. We sat down and he still wasn't talking. I finally said, 'Look, what's wrong?' and he exploded.

"'I can't do this anymore! I don't want to find the solution together, because you're the problem!'

"That's when I realized that he had taken my suggestion about coaching as an order. He's now talking to an external coach, and everything's going fine."

We call this the "gut check." Before coaching can address thorny issues—like substandard behavior—both people have to "check in" with their own feelings and thoughts to see if they really want to move forward. It's imperative that ego and power stay out of this process. Big rule: Only when people are free to say "no" can they legitimately say "yes."

Finally, if someone you're coaching decides to end the coaching process during a period of trouble, don't take it personally. As Marian Baker reminded us: "The only coaches who've never had people leave their practices are coaches who are just getting started." The same is true for manager-coaches.

Taking It Personally

A mid-sized value-added reseller in the technology field had a manager we learned a lot from. He was not a popular manager; in fact, his employees called him "Blowhard" and "Buffy" (short for "buffoon") behind his back—a reference to the long, innocuous speeches he'd give in meetings.

He was so unpopular that his boss—a senior director—put him on written warning that he needed to establish a working rapport with his subordinates, or he'd get his walking papers. "Buffy" went to several seminars over the next few weeks, all recommended by the HR rep to his division. He learned how to make friends, he learned how to resolve conflicts, and he learned to coach.

One of his employees tells the tale.

"So Buffy comes back from this seminar and calls us all into a room. 'I'm a coach now,' he echoed through the conference room. 'So I want to hear all your problems and help you achieve balance in your lives.' The actual speech lasted about ten minutes, but he didn't say anything else. We cleared out of the room as quickly as we could so he wouldn't hear us laughing. It wasn't a great day for Buffy. One person left the meeting and immediately turned Buffy in to HR for insisting that we talk to him about personal problems. Buffy didn't come back the next day."

The moral of the story is that coaching is only as strong as the real relationships between people. If you ain't real, you don't get to deal.

We interviewed another manager who had the good sense to recognize trouble and take corrective action.

"I had an employee who I just hated. I hate to say that, but just thinking about him made me tense.

"No matter how hard I tried to see his potential, or help him to develop his abilities, I just thought of him as a chump. So I sat down with him and said, 'I just don't think I can effectively coach you.'

"I wasn't surprised when he seemed relieved. I'm happy to say that he started working with an external coach and ended up taking a lateral move into another department. He's now a manager at my level."

If you're trying to coach someone who you just don't like, it's likely that the feeling's mutual, even if you think you can mask your feelings. The boundary here is that if personal feelings get in the way of your ability to "see" this person's potential, you are not the best coach for him or her.

"Hell No, We Won't Grow"

Sometimes, manager-coaches face problems so big in scope that other operations must come to a halt in order for them to address the problem at hand. We recently consulted for a company where this was the case.

This was a small company with what we thought was an excellent idea and a plan that would allow for substantial growth. We were excited to participate in helping to grow the company, and immediately began working with the Chief Operating Officer.

The COO was a charismatic, able man who spoke in such a way that we felt we had walked into a culture already operating at the "important" cultural level. Yet early on, we saw evidence that this wasn't true, and that instead, the culture was generally "ineffective" and sometimes "useful," at best. But the COO seemed to accept our advice. We even reported to the board that he was "coachable."

Strangely, though, every time the COO took our coaching and went away to accomplish some task, he would return not with the task completed, but with an explanation about why it was impossible. So while the COO talked like a citizen of an "important" culture, his work—his actions—placed him squarely in an "ineffective" culture.

Then we began to notice that other strange things were happening at this company. Deals the COO had envisioned began falling through at the last minute. There too, it was always the circumstances; the COO was never responsible for his own failures. Worse, the company's accounting system was substantially behind in handling the company's accounts. This was a cash business, but the COO never knew, on a day-to-day basis, where the company stood financially.

After a few weeks at this company, with the principal investors growing increasingly concerned (and with our own concerns rising as well), we called for an intensive, company-wide audit. The COO became deeply upset, and within a few days of the audit's commencement, he entered the office at night, deleted computer files, took printed files, took the company seal and other documents, and disappeared.

It didn't take us long to discover that the company's principal investors had been the victims of fraud. While we hadn't found direct evidence up to this point, we had seen a number of indicators, or hints, that something wasn't quite right. And it soon became apparent to us that even minor evidence of fraud is usually the tip of the fraud iceberg, and that there is almost certainly quite a bit of funny business going on beneath the surface.

The moral of this story is that coaching should lead to an almost immediate pattern of growth. (Remember that the J Curve predicts things will get worse before they get better, but then they should get better—a lot better.) If the growth always seems a step something's wrong. Either your coaching isn't working or amiss. Either way, it's probably time to dial 911 and get some help. If something is amiss, you'll be a hero for realizing it before anyone else. If your coaching was a little off, you and the subordinate will be heroes for learning and growing so quickly.

"Money, Money, Money"

What if people are complaining a lot about money? At first glance, this might seem to be a "many hats, one head" problem. How can you coach the person to go for their goals when at the same time you're the one who denies big raises because you don't see the performance gains yet?

First of all, there's ample evidence to suggest that people don't work just for the money, and that instead, people seek personal satisfaction, emotional fulfillment, and "self-actualization" from work. Unless they are grossly underpaid, people won't likely consider money as a primary factor in their reasons for staying at or leaving a particular job.[1]

In a situation like this, listening is vital. It's possible that they're using one complaint (money) to cover what's really important. It's also possible that money is what's really important. At first glance, it's tough to tell the difference.

Somewhere in there, they have requests for action that could be turned into "contracts." But before they'll voice those requests, they're going to need to be heard. And to do that, they'll have to trust that the person who's listening, is actually listening.

If you find yourself in this situation of coaching your direct reports about money, tread carefully. You can't go wrong by listening (refer back to the "going deep" principle). If money does turn out to be the problem, you might find yourself in confusion of roles. If this does happen, dialing 911 is not a bad plan. As Martha Stewart says, "It's a good thing."

Problems, What Problems?

If there's a system-wide problem in your organization, it's a good idea to figure out what it is, why it's there, and what to do about it before you start coaching your people.

One of the big warning signs of a problem is that executives aren't willing to talk about problems. Sounds weird but it is true. If all the news is good news, watch out.

Employee turnover is another barometer of trouble. After the Dutch insurance and banking giant ING bought British merchant bank and stockbroker Barings PLC in 1995, employees gave the Dutch chairman, Hessel Lindenbergh, a standing ovation.[2] But by the middle of 1996, more than sixty members of Barings's Latin American equities team had left. Lindenbergh suggests that the defections weren't ruinous to the company. Still, replacing workers is never inexpensive, particularly when they're highly skilled and well paid. So what's a manager-coach to do in a situation like this?

The turnover at ING Barings represents something of an extreme. That's why we can learn from it. Most managers will know quickly when turnover picks up, and if they're paying close attention, they'll recognize signs that increased turnover might be on the horizon. A manager-coach in this or a similar situation might have understood that behind people's gripes about their new company, there were probably numerous requests that went unheard. Digging out the requests for action behind the griping, and then crafting some methods to manage the contracts that arise from those requests might be one possible answer here. This might also be an appropriate time for an intelligent manager-coach to look for some outside help to diagnose the problem.

If You're Not a High Achiever, Stop Reading

So far, we've covered the big warning signs that might cause you to seek outside help. Our analogy—which we've probably beaten to death by now—is the ER room. Dial 911.

There's another, more empowered analogy. People generally see doctors for two reasons—they are sick (the ER reason) or they want to get as healthy as they can.

Many of the external coaches and internal manager-coaches we talked with advised that the biggest reason to get outside help is to make sure the coaching gets completely drilled into the culture. Marian Baker, the Chicago coach, said that, "My vision is that managers work with coaches and get coaching down to their bones. Then they can become advocates for corporate-wide coaching."

Brian Kritzell, a California-based coach, suggested a "coach in residence" program, similar to the role organizational psychologists sometimes play. This is a person who is physically in the company but is external, and works under an agreement of confidentiality. Anyone can see this coach for any reason (up to a certain number of visits). It's a great way to mix the benefits of outside coaching with the benefits of manager-coaches.

Kevin Cashman, author of *Leadership from the Inside Out* and CEO of LeaderSource, told us about his company's approach to developing world-class coaching in companies. Corporate leaders participate in an intensive program with his firm in which they focus on four key areas: personal mastery, interpersonal mastery, career mastery, and life balance. Notice the word "mastery." That's what world-class leaders are interested in.

In each area, the corporate leaders create teams of coaches to make sure they become practicing experts in each area. When the leaders return to their companies, they go back with a top-notch support structure in place. As their understanding of coaching deepens, their ability to coach their direct reports increases. "It's a way of ensuring that coaching really takes hold," he noted. "People go from tolerating problems to actively transforming them. It's inspiring to watch."

Role Clarification

If you choose to bring in outside coaches, make sure everyone concerned understands why. All the coaches we interviewed argued that clarity about the coaching program is an absolute must or it will look bogus.

Jim Beasley, a coach we've mentioned several times, summed up the issue this way: "Everyone, from the president to the janitor, has got to know why I'm there. If they don't, I can't do my job."

Evaluation

If you do decide to bring someone in, make sure they don't stay too long. We're not arguing for short-duration coaching, we're arguing for value-added consulting. Sadly, many consultants—and some coaches—try to create dependencies that ensure they'll be coming back.

We started this chapter by telling you about our end-of-the-year tradition. We suggest you have a similar tradition—to talk about all your consultants. If they're not adding value, or if you feel they should win the "consultant most deserving to have a novel written about them award," it's probably time to rethink their contract.

There is a lot of good help out there. By following the principles in this chapter, you'll know when to get good help—and make sure the help stays good.

chapter fifteen

Coaching Across
the Generations

Today, the popular business press is abuzz with generational lingo—
"Gen X commercial hits," "Gen Y marketing disasters," "Boomer retirement plans," "Boomlet career expectations," and so on. We've been
talking about generational issues for almost ten years—so long that we
have archived PowerPoint slides titled "What's a Gen Xer?" that we'd
show to explain these obscure concepts to audiences that would often
seem puzzled.

Back in the early '90s, we'd discuss the popular stereotypes about
Generation X: "slackers," "overachievers," "Gordon Gekkos," and
"dropouts," which we argued were contradictory.

The use of stereotypes continues to puzzle us. Not the fact that it
happens, because people have always stereotyped one another. What we
find surprising is that educated, informed audiences will sit still when a
not-so-informed talking head at a seminar says: "And Gen Xers are . . ."
followed by a list of adjectives. The same audience would probably boo
or hiss if John Rocker repeated his stereotype-dripping critique of New
York. Although people today won't tolerate stereotyping of most groups,

they will look for stereotypes about the generations and they'll even pay a lot of money to hear lists of "how the Boomers act."

To look at it positively, stereotyping is often the first step as one group tries to understand another. Thankfully, we don't stay in this step for long. Not so many generations ago, African-Americans were commonly stereotyped by a list of adjectives. Then, in the 1970s, the same people who held these beliefs watched the popular TV miniseries *Roots* and saw that African-Americans, like any other group, have a history in this country and in Africa, and that this history gives them a richness and a complexity that a stereotype can't begin to capture. As a society, we're still working on race relations—and we have a long way to go. But *Roots* was a milestone—and a positive one—toward our progress.

The purpose of this chapter is twofold. First, it will bring our thinking about the generations past the level of stereotypes and up to the level of grasping the richness and complexity of each group. Second, it will focus on coaching techniques that will bridge the generational divide.

The benefits of bringing the generations together at work are enormous. For the first time in American history, major corporations have four generations—from the World War II seniors to "Generation Y" just now beginning internships—working side by side. *Wow.* Managers who can understand and appreciate the differences will be able to build more effective teams, attract and retain talent in each of the generations, resolve conflicts faster, and build organizations that welcome the contributions from each group.

Challenger vs. Moonwalk[1]

Coauthor Dave Logan was a senior in high school when the *Challenger* exploded. Like most Generation Xers, it didn't mean much to him when it happened. Looking back, though, it was one of those events that epitomized a time in America. It was a clarifying moment in our history. The economy was good, hopes for jobs were strong, the United States seemed to be winning the Cold War, but like for most people in Generation X, things didn't feel as good as they looked. Divorce rates in America were at record highs. Both parents working created the "latchkey kid" phenomenon.

While Dave's parents were (and are) still married, it seemed that the system was somehow letting the entire generation of Xers down—while their parents didn't necessarily put them last, they weren't first, either. Breakdowns in the educational system caused many in the media to ask, "Why can't Johnny read?"

When the *Challenger* exploded, it seemed to somehow represent what was already happening to this generation—a series of mistakes, a few people putting their careers ahead of their commitments to safety, some incompetence, all mixed with tragic results. The mission should have been routine, but something went wrong. *Challenger* took Christa McAuliffe, the woman who represented our teachers, with it. *Challenger* captures a moment—the "system" seems to be working well, but somehow it had left us behind when people in power put their needs ahead of ours. This moment captured the essence of Generation X, people born between 1965 and 1988.[2]

Contrast *Challenger* with the first moonwalk in 1969. In the midst of a world gone mad with race riots, the antiwar movement at its zenith, government and industry came together behind the vision of an American president. Kennedy was long since assassinated, but the dream went on without him. According to some sociologists, Neil Armstrong's walk on the moon epitomized the vision of a generation—business working with researchers, hand-in-hand with the government, to produce the first human moonwalk. The symbol of this event captured the imagination of the Baby Boomers, the group born between 1946 and 1964.

What these two events have in common is that they happened as one generation was making its way from childhood to adulthood. In both cases, the symbol captured the flavor of how people were experiencing life—a flavor that has changed little.

Challenger was greeted by Gen Xers as a confirmation of what they already knew: "The system that seemed to be working had let us down." A few years after *Challenger*, another landmark event affected Generation X: the recession of the early '90s—the time when the oldest in this group were graduating from college. Headlines at the time declared a dearth of "real" jobs, but lots of "McJobs." As a generation, "The feeling we had is that we've done what we're supposed to do, but the system is letting us down."

Generation Xers responded in a variety of ways—some stayed in school and earned advanced degrees. Others moved back in with Mom or Dad to wait. Some notched their ambition up to meet the challenges of the times. Others still found unique ways to express themselves (as often happens during times of social stress), turning to fads like body piercing or tattooing. Unfortunately, some people in the media tried to hang a single label on Generation X based on what a few people did. Most in Generation X find these labels (and the title "Gen X" itself) insulting.[3]

Yet these events did affect Generation X in somewhat consistent ways. The group's outlook became more cynical than young adults a few years earlier. Many in the group latched onto the idea of self-reliance—"No one is going to save me but me," to quote one phrase from the time.

With the Baby Boomers, the reaction shows the same process, but with a different flavor. Because authority figures seemed either good or bad, the Boomers developed a love/hate attitude toward government and politics. Many in the group also became idealistic, believing that a better world could be created despite the abuses of power demonstrated in the Kent State shootings and in Watergate.

Interestingly, the other two major generations—Generation Y and the Matures—also have their landmark events. For the Matures (also called the World War II generation), or those born between 1909 and 1945, the Depression and the war framed the flavor of this group. Like the Boomers, the Matures found strength in coming together—first to survive the economic hardships, and then to fight in Africa, Europe, and the Pacific Rim. While every reaction to these events was different, a common theme developed—that fulfilling a duty leads to a better world. This generation became perhaps the hardest working in American history.

For Generation Y, we still don't know a lot, but we can make some informed guesses. First, Generation Y is leaving college with the best economy in history, so it's predictable that their expectations will be high. A recent poll in *Newsweek* supported this view.[4] Second, Gen Y is the most technically proficient generation in history. Just as happened to Gen X, this proficiency will put them at the center of attention as technology continues to shift the business landscape and our lives.

Early indications say that Generation Y will be powerful. The biggest demographic group since the Boomers, this age range is already flexing their muscle in their choice of products and services.[5] Marketers are quickly realizing that Generation Y doesn't care for endorsements of stars—they want products made for them. Nike is just one company to lose significant market share by not adapting quickly enough. Some analysts are wondering if Gap and MTV (two marketing giants) can appeal to them any better. More important to readers of this book, it appears that Generation Y will be more selective in their choice of employers than Gen X. It also seems that their expectations of promotion and increases in compensation are also higher.

Since the two largest groups in today's workforce are the Boomers and Gen X, we'll continue to explore how these generations are different, and how they're alike. Then we'll discuss coaching techniques to bring everyone at work together.

Walter Cronkite vs. *anything.com*

We can hardly talk about Generation X without talking about the tremendous amounts of information at their disposal.

Boomers had a few "credible" sources of information—Walter Cronkite, the *New York Times*, the *Washington Post*. If it came from any of these sources, it was part of the national agenda. As most Boomers would quickly point out, just because it came from Walter Cronkite's lips didn't make it trustworthy, but it did make it important.

The relatively few sources of information united the Boomers around a common set of issues, such as the Vietnam War, education, the draft, the environment, the power of companies, the Cold War, and the future of international cooperation. The Boomers had many different reactions to these issues (as is true of any generation), but the issues to which they responded were largely similar.

With hundreds of cable channels, even more bulletin boards, and the Internet, Xers live in a different world. A poll a few years ago suggested that more Xers believe in UFOs than believe Social Security will be there when they're ready to retire. How's that for a generational credibility gap? To some in the media, this suggests a lack of education. Far from it, we believe the opposite is true—it suggests that Generation X's informational database is fed by an extremely wide variety of information sources, from the credible to the ridiculous. A recent poll of the favorite TV shows of Xers revealed that almost none are on the three major U.S. networks—and many are on remote cable stations, such as Comedy Central.

The contrast is that Boomers were quick to evaluate the few sources of information that were available to them. Xers, on the other hand, were quick to find new sources of information. This is hugely significant. Generation X stereotypes the Boomers as not being up on what's happening. Boomers believe that Xers can't think critically. Like any stereotype, both are based only on partial truths. To put it positively, Xers are the most informed generation in history, while Boomers are perhaps the most discriminating. Xers and Ys amaze their professors with their ability to find information on any topic (including whole research papers posted to the Web), while Boomer professors amaze their younger students with their ability to show logical gaps, flaws in reasoning, and erroneous assumptions. To put it simplistically, Xers are great at finding data, while Boomers are great at turning it into information.

Again, though, neither stereotype is true of everyone. Many Gen Xers and Ys growing up in poor areas have not had cable TV or Internet access. And many Boomers are as proficient on the Internet as their younger counterparts.

In general, though, we see a lot of similarities running through all the generations: each group uses its strengths to address the concerns of the day. For the Boomers, these are its size, its ability to critique information, and its resolve in getting things done. For the Xers, these are its ability to reinvent itself (as evidenced by the "slacker" stereotype turning into the "IPO millionaires" label) and its talent at working with new technology.

All in the Family vs. *South Park*

Just as *All in the Family* explained the generation gap between the Matures and Boomers, *South Park* explains the gap between Boomers and Xers. Both shows pushed the envelope in their day. Both took on serious issues with a sense of humor. Both caused many people in the older generation to switch off the TV.

In contrast to multiple Emmy Award–winning *All in the Family*, *South Park* is well out of the mainstream. *All in the Family* was on a major TV network, while *South Park* is on Comedy Central.

Both shows, however, will be remembered as being popular among their generations. Both highlight the differences between the generations and describe the issues in that generation's words.

In *All in the Family*, Meathead was a Boomer, Archie a Mature. Each represents stereotypes of their generation's outlook. To Archie, the key was to work hard, stay in line, and not mess up the system that's worked so far. To Meathead, the system was corrupt, Archie was narrow-minded, and people didn't spend enough time thinking.

Even though *South Park*'s heroes are kids in elementary school, they really represent Xers and their outlook. Interestingly, all the adults on *South Park* are either self-centered, insane, stupid, or all of the above. The teacher, Mr. Garrison, believes he is respected and adored by the kids, but in reality the kids think he is a buffoon. There is only one adult the kids trust—the school chef—whom they call, Chef. He is not educated, has no title (other than Chef), and is not a moral pillar. So why do the children like him? They like him because, unlike their parents, Chef is competent and puts them first. More importantly, he cares with his actions, not just with his words.

To a group that was fortunate in materialistic ways but that felt under-parented, *South Park* resonates. To a group that wanted a truly better world in which people would align around a vision, *All in the Family* feels familiar.

What *South Park* Says about Xer Values

Recently, coauthor Dave Logan spoke to a large group of police officers—most of whom were in plain clothes but with very visible, very large guns. Getting distracted by all the firepower, he finally stopped in the middle of his presentation and said, "That's a very large gun you have there. I'm not sure someone of your size needs such a large weapon." After the laughter died down in the room, the officer shared a story of when he was walking down the street in a neighborhood with a dense Gen X population. No one seemed concerned or impressed by the fact that he was there. They weren't even interested in what he was doing there. Their expressions almost seemed to say "And you're here because . . . ?"

This infuriated the officer. As he told the story, he said: "I felt like saying, 'I'm a cop—aren't you nervous?'" Police departments around the country are learning that power and authority are not enough with Generation X.[6]

The very word "authority" was ridiculed in an entire episode of *South Park*. When one of the kids (a representative of Gen X) had to fill in for the inept adult police force, the authority went to his head in an insane and megalomaniacal way.

Authority figures let them down when they left them as latchkey kids to fend for themselves, when they didn't get the jobs they felt they were entitled to because of the recession of the early '90s which the authority figures themselves caused. And even though the recession is long over and the Xers have enjoyed the greatest job and financial boom in history, they are still operating like they don't/can't trust their parents. As a result, the most talented and prepared population demographic in history has entered the corporate workforce with a major chip on its shoulder.

It isn't authority that they respect; it's competence, no matter what the person's level. They think more of a competent janitor than an incompetent vice president. In the case of *South Park*, it's a competent Chef.

If your authority as a manager is derived from status, then you, like the teacher Mr. Garrison, may not be reaching this generation. Generation X respects authority based upon competence and sincere concern for them as individuals. Having grown up with divorce more than any other generation in history, it is long-term relationships they're after.

Instead of using your positional power, "I'm the boss so you should listen to me" (this is no doubt a gross exaggeration), a more effective approach would be, "I've found in my experience . . . I hope this is useful to you."

This is how Chef deals with the kids in *South Park*. His approach appeals to their need for long-term relationships and their desire to establish competence before passing out advice. We now turn to how today's manager-coaches can use an understanding of the differences and similarities of generational groups to reach everyone in today's workforce.

What's Really the Same

Whether we're talking about how the Matures responded to the Nazi threat, or how Generation Y is adapting to new technology, the processes people use to make sense of their environments are the same. In each case, the important events of the day left the young people with a perspective. As this group matured, this perspective changed slightly, but the needs of people are universal.

In one of our recent workshops, the general counsel of a major corporation made the following observation: it's ironic that people try to express their individuality in the same ways. He stumbled onto one of the fundamental needs that cuts vividly across generational lines: people want to be understood as individuals, not by their reputations or their stereotypes. Sadly, many managers leave workshops on Gen X, honestly believing that they now understand "this group" (as if the individual doesn't matter).

Recently, a 25-year-old (Generation X) employee of a manufacturing company sat down in one of our seminars. As he entered the room, every person watched him. More specifically, they looked at his body piercings, his tattoos, and his hair (which was a purple version of Ricky Martin's). It was fascinating to observe people's reactions to him. Most whispered quietly. The people at his table ignored him. He, of course, looked uncomfortable.

Then some guy in his forties did this brilliant thing. He got up, walked over to him, shook his hand and said: "Your tattoos are great! What do they mean?" The now-gleaming Gen Xer explained that he was in the marines for three years, and that's when he got his first tattoo, then he dated a girl named "Yesenia" (the same name etched in his forearm), and so on. After he'd been recognized as an individual, he was more outgoing and expressive.

Two years later, we visited that same company, and saw Tom (the painted person) again. His tattoos were still there, but his haircut looked like something from a Young Republicans rally. More striking was his overall appearance—an in-style, upscale, corporately correct presentation. In asking what had happened, he told us that the person who had first introduced himself (Chuck) had become his designated mentor in the company. Once Chuck got in with Tom, he coached him by saying that he used to have a haircut that everyone complained about, and it really held him back. Tom said he'd always known his look would change, and he chose that moment for the transformation. Tom appreciated

Chuck's genuine interest in him. Chuck appreciated who Tom could be with a little coaching.

What interested us was that Chuck first recognized Tom as an individual *before* giving advice—just as Chef in *South Park* does with the kids. This is an effective way of coaching Generation X. In fact, it's an effective way of coaching *everyone*.

The universal truth this points to is that people want to be recognized and validated for who they are before people suggest an alteration. Great manager-coaches use their first meetings with people to establish this level of rapport. They show that their employees are understood before "fixing" them. Coaching is not about fixing, it's about bringing out people's potential.

The other universal truth the "generations" discussion brings up is that everyone *really* is value-driven, even though people's values are different. Many Boomers began to value "honesty" and "equality" above all else during the civil rights movement, the antiwar protests, and Watergate. When the Boomers ascended to positions of power, they wrote the Freedom of Information Act into law.

In a similar fashion, the Generation Xers value "competence" and "self-reliance" more than other generations, perhaps because these two factors made a difference during the recession of the early '90s. Today, many Gen Xers are anti-affirmative action, even though many of the same people are for greater spending of education dollars in impoverished areas.

We draw artificial lines between the generations by saying that what we value is different. The point is, we all value things, and we want these values to be central in our lives and in our work. The task of the manager-coach, then, is twofold: to probe into everyone's values and to help them build their careers around what's important to them.

Across generations, "freedom," "opportunity," and "feedback on performance" seem to be important to everyone.[7]

The Differences That Matter

But to say "everyone's really the same" without a big footnote would be a mistake. The fact is that each generation is different in what it values. In general, Boomers value accomplishment more than Xers. Matures value duty more than either Boomers or Ys.

One of the big differences between Boomers and Matures is the degree to which Boomers value team process. When Boomers looked for work, they sought out companies that put teams at the center. Companies that didn't adapt to the flood of Boomers didn't attract or retain the top talent. Many of the "best" companies in the 1960s are not around any more, largely because they didn't adapt to the needs of a changing workforce.

Xers are climbing the corporate ladder in companies today, just as Boomers did a generation ago. Those companies that recognize and adapt to the differences are finding that Xers are breaking the "no loyalty" stereotype by building their futures in one company.

At a recent retreat of a large financial services company, we heard what many of the older Generation Xers and the younger Boomers said when no one powerful was listening. The discussion was almost universal: if this company doesn't figure out work/life balance, we won't stay another five years. Perhaps most frightening for this company is that the people attending the retreat were the designated leaders for the next *two decades*.

According to several studies, Xer values tend to include:

- A sense of belongingness
- Teamwork, linked to competence and diversity
- Ability to learn new things
- Recognition of individual differences
- Short-term rewards

For manager-coaches, we recommend two key actions to make your company, large or small, a great place for Xers—and Ys behind them—to build their careers. The first is to probe into the values of younger people in your workforce. The tools in this book will help. We suggest you "blur your eyes" to see what the common values in this group are.

The second is to convene a cross-generational, cross-functional team to ask four simple questions:

- In what ways are the practices and policies of this company aligned with these values?
- In what ways are the practices and policies of this company not aligned with these values?
- So what?
- Now what?

One large insurance company investigated these questions and realized its policies and practices did not support two key values of Generation X in its workforce: work/life balance, and rapid promotion. In thinking about work/life balance, the company leaders wrestled with how to implement this. In the end, they decided not to change anything—because that company's tradition was based on people giving their lives to the company. Despite our suggestions to focus on work/life balance, the company decided that it would attract and retain people who, like the present leaders, valued accomplishment over balance.

Four years later, the strategy seems to be paying off for them. Despite the labor crunch, they've had almost no problem getting great people. They did make one key change, though—they advertise the company as a place where "wimps need not apply." The honesty in advertising has paid off—they stumbled into another Xer value: honesty without hype.

You may decide to change everything because of Gen X values, or you may decide to change nothing. We suggest that your choice should be an informed one, just as it was for this company.

Pulling It All Together

In the end, we're back to where we started—listen to people and they'll tell you who they are. Listening requires care and commitment. It also requires patience. In the end, great coaches are ones who "listen" people into greatness by helping them align their practices with what's important to them.

Yet manager-coaches take one additional step: they "listen" the company into greatness by aligning it with the values of their people. Manager-coach is a way of life and an unfolding process. We wish you well as you discover your own pathway to being a great manager-coach. Let us know how it's going.

Endnotes

Chapter 1

1. A history of coaching from the 1960s on can be found in Frederic Hudson's *The Handbook of Coaching* (San Francisco: Jossey-Bass, 1999).
2. Joshua Hyatt, "The Zero-Defect CEO," *Inc.*, June 1997, p. 46.

Part I

1. Joan Haslip, *Marie Antoinette* (New York: Weidenfeld & Nicolson, 1987), p. 303.

Chapter 2

1. "Just Do It! But How?" *Chief Executive*, May 1995, p. 22.
2. This belief is one of the foundations for the field of "rhetoric," which predates both medicine and logic in ancient Greece. For a good explanation of filters at work, read Kenneth Burke's "Terministic Screens" essay in *Language as Symbolic Action: Essays on Life, Literature, and Method* (Berkeley: University of California, 1966).
3. Roger D'Aprix, Karen Greenbaum, and Gloria Gordon, "Senior Executives and Corporate Communicators, Wake Up!" *Communication World*, 14, no. 8 (Aug/Sept 1997): p. 39–44.
4. "Listening from" and "listening for" central ideas of Theodor Reik's *Listening with the Third Ear: The Inner Experiences of a Psychoanalyst* (Straus and Company, 1949). "Listening for" is also a seminal theme in self psychology, as explained by founder Heinz Kohut in *Analysis of the Self* (International Universities Press, 1971).

5. For a good review of active listening, see *Organizational Communication: Balancing Creativity and Constraint,* by Eric Eisenberg and H. K. Goodall, Jr. (New York: St. Martin's Press, 1993), p. 253–255.
6. H. Ross Perot, "Business Leaders: It's Up to Us to Recover the Industrial Leadership," in *The Book of Leadership Wisdom: Classic Writings by Legendary Business Leaders,* ed. Peter Krass (New York: John Wiley & Sons, 1998).

Chapter 3

1. W. Sapir, *Language: An Introduction to the Study of Speech* (New York: Harcourt, Brace & World, 1921).
2. Martin Heidegger (1889–1976), "Building Dwelling Thinking," lecture, 5 August 1951, published in *Poetry, Language, Thought.* Translation and introduction by Albert Hofstadter. (New York: Harper & Row, 1971).
3. K. Burke, *Language As Symbolic Action: Essays on Life, Literature, and Method* (Berkeley: University of California, 1966).

Chapter 4

1. Jacques Lacan, *The Four Fundamental Concepts of Psychoanalysis* (New York: W.W. Norton & Co, 1998).
2. Harold S. Geneen, "Leadership," in *The Book of Leadership Wisdom: Classic Writings by Legendary Business Leaders,* ed. Peter Krass (New York: John Wiley & Sons, 1998).

Chapter 5

1. Bennett Daviss, "Profits from Principle: Five Forces Redefining Business," *The Futurist,* March 1999, p. 38–44.
2. Karl Weick, *Sensemaking in Organizations* (Sage, 1995).
3. Michael Moeller and Victoria Murphy, "Outta Here at Microsoft," *BusinessWeek,* November 29, 1999, p. 156–160.
4. Michelle Conlin and Peter Coy, "The Wild New Workforce," *BusinessWeek,* December 6, 1999, p. 38–44.
5. Meg Lundstrom, "'Mommy, Do You Love Your Company More Than Me?'" *BusinessWeek,* December 20, 1999, p. 175.
6. Larry Greiner, "Evolution and Revolution as Organizations Grow," *Harvard Business Review* 50, 1972, p. 37–46.
7. Donna Fenn, "Domestic Policy," *Inc.,* November 1999, p. 38–45.
8. Michelle Conlin, "Religion in the Workplace: The Growing Presence of Spirituality in Corporate America," *BusinessWeek,* November 1, 1999, p. 151–158.
9. Ibid.
10. For a free LifeLine package that will evaluate your satisfaction with your most important work/life regions, and map these onto the five cultures, visit our web site at *www.coachingrevolution.com.* This package will also coach you to develop your own personal initiatives, mentioned later in this chapter.

Part II

1. Ira Sager, "Inside IBM: Internet Business Machines," *BusinessWeek,* December 13, 1999, p. EB20–EB40.

Chapter 6

1. Ludwig Wittgenstein, *Tractatus Logico-Philosophicus* (London: Routledge & Kegan Paul, 1922).
2. John Searle, *Speech Acts: An Essay in the Philosophy of Language* (Cambridge: Cambridge University Press, 1969); Negel Love, "Searle on Language," *Language & Communication,* 19, no. 1 (1999): p. 9–25.
3. Norman Malcolm, *Ludwig Wittgenstein: A Memoir* (London: Oxford University Press, 1958).
4. For example, "The Role of Political Language Forms and Language Coherence in the Organizational Change Process," by John Sillince, *Organization Studies,* 20, no. 3 (1999): p. 485–519.
5. Leslie Helm, "Turmoil at Apple: Something Went Awry—But What Is Debatable," *The Los Angeles Times,* February 3, 1996, p. 3.
6. Theodore Roosevelt, Speech before the Hamilton Club, Chicago, April 10, 1899.
7. George Bernard Shaw, "In the Beginning," *Back to Methuselah,* Act 1 (New York: The Limited Editions Club, 1939).
8. Harold S. Geneen, "Leadership," in *The Book of Leadership Wisdom: Classic Writings by Legendary Business Leaders,* ed. Peter Krass (New York: John Wiley & Sons, 1998).
9. Robert D. Hass, "Ethics: A Global Challenge," in *The Book of Leadership Wisdom: Classic Writings by Legendary Business Leaders,* ed. Peter Krass (New York: John Wiley & Sons, 1998).

Chapter 7

1. From a recent interview with ABC News.
2. An excellent analysis of the Cendant crisis, and lessons learned, appeared in the article "The Cendant Mess Gets Messier," by Amy Barrett and Jennifer Reingold, *BusinessWeek,* August 3, 1998, p. 68–71.
3. Forest McDonald, *The Presidency of George Washington* (Lawrence: University of Kansas Press, 1998).
4. Ben Cohen and Jerry Greenfield, "Lead with Your Values," in *The Book of Leadership Wisdom: Classic Writings by Legendary Business Leaders,* ed. Peter Krass (New York: John Wiley & Sons, 1998).

Chapter 8

1. Karen Robinson, "The Role of Nursing in the Influenza Epidemic of 1918–1919," *Nursing Forum,* 25, no. 2 (1990): p. 19–26.
2. Sigmund Freud, *Jokes and Their Relation to the Unconscious* (New York: W. W. Norton & Co., 1963).
3. Charles R. Bantz, *Understanding Organizations: Interpreting Organizational Communication Cultures* (Columbia, S.C.: University of South Carolina Press, 1993).
4. Tim Carvell, "By the Way . . . Your Staff Hates You" *Fortune,* September 28, 1998, p. 200–212.
5. Abraham Maslow, *Maslow on Management* (New York: John Wiley & Sons, 1998).
6. Thomas Cummings and Christopher G. Worley, *Organization Development and Change,* 6th ed. (Cincinnati, Ohio: South-Western College Publishing, 1997).
7. J.D. Ford and L.W. Ford, "The Role of Conversations in Producing Intentional Change in Organizations," *Academic Management Review,* 20, no. 3 (1995): p. 541–70.
8. Terry Winograd and Fernando Flores, *Understanding Computers and Cognition: A New Foundation for Design* (Boston: Addison-Wesley, 1995).

9. Aristotle, *The Rhetoric*.
10. Michael Lombardo and Robert Eichinger, *Eighty-eight Assignments for Development in Place: Enhancing the Developmental Challenge of Existing Jobs* (Greensboro: Center for Creative Leadership, 1989); Beverly Kaye and Sharon Jordan-Evans, *Love 'Em or Lose 'Em: Getting Good People to Stay* (San Francisco: Berrett-Koehler, 1999).
11. Norma D'Annunzio-Green and John Macandrew, "Re-empowering the Empowered—The Ultimate Challenge?" *Personnel Review*, 28, no. 3 (1999): p. 258–278.
12. Robert Slater, *Get Better or Get Beaten: 31 Leadership Secrets from GE's Jack Welch* (Burr Ridge, Illinois: Irwin Professional Publications, 1994).

Part III

1. Leonardo Da Vinci, *Notebooks*, circa 1500.

Chapter 9

1. Emily Thornton, with Larry Armstrong, Katie Kerwin, and Inka Resch, "A New Order at Nissan," *BusinessWeek*, October 11, 1999, p. 54–55.
2. Samuel C. Certo, *Principles of Modern Management: Functions and Systems* (Dubuque, Iowa: William C. Brown Publishers, 1983), p. 199.
3. Seanna Browder, "Great Service Wasn't Enough," *BusinessWeek*, April 19, 1999, p. 126–127.
4. Jonathan Moore with Mia Trinephi, "Taipei's Subway Project Is Way Off Track," *BusinessWeek* (Int'l edition), June 24, 1996, p. 154–157.
5. Charles Fishman, "Sanity Inc." *First Company*, January 1999, p. 84.
6. Lew Platt, "Lew Platt's Fix-It Plan for Hewlett Packard," *BusinessWeek* July 13, 1998, p. 128–131.

Chapter 10

1. John A. Byrne, "The Best and Worst Boards," *BusinessWeek*, January 24, 2000, p. 146.
2. Amy Barrett and Jennifer Reingold, "The Cendant Mess Gets Messier," *BusinessWeek*, August 3, 1998, p. 68–71.
3. T.J. Dermot Dunphy, "LBOs Didn't Make Formica Lose Its Gloss," *BusinessWeek*, April 19, 1999, p. 12.
4. Jennifer Reingold, with Mica Schneider and Kerry Capell, "Learning to Lead," *BusinessWeek*, October 18, 1999, p. 76.

Chapter 11

1. William B. Brenneman, J. Bernard Keys, and Robert M. Fulmer, "Learning Across a Living Company: The Shell Companies' Experiences," *Organizational Dynamics*, Autumn, 1998.
2. James C. Collins and Jerry I. Porras, *Built to Last: Successful Habits of Visionary Companies* (New York: HarperBusiness, 1997).

Part IV

Chapter 12

1. M. Landry, "A Note on the Concept of Problem," *Organization Studies*, 16 (1995): p. 15–31.
2. Karl E. Weick, "Managerial Thought in the Context of Action," *The Executive Mind*. (San Francisco: Jossey-Bass, 1983).
3. John Dewey, *How We Think* (Boston: DC Heath, 1933).
4. Based on research cited in *The Psychology of Attitudes* by Alice Eagly and Shelly Chaiken (Fort Worth: Harcourt Brace Jovanovich College Publishers, 1993); see also "How Senior Managers Think" by Daniel Isenberg in *Harvard Business Review*, vol. 62 (1984): p. 81–90. Freud identified the same pattern in his extensive investigation of the unconscious.
5. From Scheef Organizational Development and Training.
6. Patricia Ward Biederman and Warren G. Bennis, *Organizing Genius: The Secrets of Creative Collaboration* (Reading, Massachusetts: Addison-Wesley, 1997).
7. Thomas Kuhn, *Structure of Scientific Revolutions* (University of Chicago, 1996).
8. Q. Spitzer and R. Evans, "New Problems in Problem-Solving," *Across the Board*, 34 (1995): p. 30–36.
9. We are indebted to Beverly Kaye for sparking this idea.
10. M. Cohen, J. March, and J. Olsen, "A Garbage Can Model of Organizational Choice," *Administrative Science Quarterly* 17 (1972): p. 1–25.

Chapter 13

1. Andrew Wilson, "Russian Military Haunted by Past Glories: Battle to Improve Slumping Morale and Poor Performance," *Jane's International Defence Review*, May 1, 1996.
2. Elisabeth Kübler-Ross, *On Death and Dying* (New York: Scribner Classics, 1997).
3. Ibid.
4. D. Kolb, *Experiential Learning: Experience as the Source of Learning and Development* (Englewood Cliffs, NJ: Prentice Hall, 1984).

Chapter 14

1. For more information on this point, see Beverly Kaye and Sharon Jordan-Evans's *Love 'Em or Lose 'Em: Getting Good People to Stay* (Berrett-Koehler, 1999).
2. Julia Flynn, et. al, "The Brain Drain at ING Barings," *BusinessWeek*, July 8, 1996.

Chapter 15

1. The idea that generations form their identity because of landmark events is based partially on Bob Losyk's "Generation X: What They Think and What They Plan to Do" in *The Futurist*, March-April 1997.
2. The dates that delineate Boomers, Generation X, and Generation Y vary from author to author. These dates are based on analysis presented in Walker Smith and Ann Clurman's *Rocking the Generations: The Yankelovich Report on Generational Marketing* (HarperBusiness, 1997).

3. For more information on these attitudes, and why they formed, see Geoffrey Holtz's *Welcome to the Jungle: The Why Behind 'Generation X'* (New York, St. Martin's Press, 1995), and William Strauss and Neil Howe's *Generations: The History of America's Future, 1584–2069* (New York: William Morrow, 1992).
4. See the May 8, 2000 issue of *Newsweek* for several excellent articles and poll data about Generation Y.
5. Ellen Neuborne and Kathleen Kerwin, "Generation Y," *BusinessWeek*, Feb 15, 1999.
6. Bernard J. Wolfson, "Younger Workers Recharge with Play at Work," *Orange County Register,* July 12, 1999.
7. C. L. Jurkiewicz and R. G. Brown, "Gen Xers vs. Boomers vs. Matures: Generational Comparisons of Public Employee Motivation," *Review of Public Personnel Administration,* Fall, 1998.

Index